CURRIES

CURRIES

Over 200 great recipes

hamlyn

An Hachette Livre UK Company
www.hachettelivre.co.uk

First published in Great Britain in 2008 by Hamlyn,
a division of Octopus Publishing Group Ltd,
2--4 Heron Quays, London E14 4JP
www.octopusbooks.co.uk

ISBN: 978-0-600-61733-4

A CIP catalogue record for this book is available from the
British Library

Printed and bound in China

10 9 8 7 6 5 4 3 2 1

Notes

This book includes dishes made with nuts and nut derivatives. It
is advisable for those with known allergic reactions to nuts and
nut derivatives and those who may be potentially vulnerable to
these allergies, such as pregnant and nursing mothers, invalids,
the elderly, babies and children, to avoid dishes made with nuts
and nut oils. It is also prudent to check the labels of preprepared
ingredients for the possible inclusion of nut derivatives.

The Department of Health advises that eggs should not be
consumed raw. This book contains some dishes made with raw
or lightly cooked eggs. It is prudent for more vulnerable people,
such as pregnant and nursing mothers, invalids, the elderly,
babies and young children, to avoid uncooked or lightly cooked
dishes made with eggs.

Meat and poultry should be cooked thoroughly. To test if poultry
is cooked, pierce the flesh through the thickest part with a
skewer or fork – the juices should run clear, never pink or red.

Both metric and imperial measurements are given for the
recipes. Use one set of measures only, not a mixture of both.

Ovens should be preheated to the specified temperature. If using
a fan-assisted oven, follow the manufacturer's instructions for
adjusting the time and temperature. Grills should also be
preheated.

Fresh herbs should be used unless otherwise stated.

Figures given for preparation and cooking times
('Prep' and 'Cook') are given in minutes.

contents

introduction

Despite curry being one of the most popular meals in the West, most people never attempt to cook a curry dish from scratch due to a perception that the recipes are time consuming and complicated and contain lots of ingredients that are not readily available in supermarkets. Well, this book is here to dispel all of these myths and to introduce you to a variety of wonderfully fragrant, delicious homemade dishes that don't require any specialist cooking skills or hours of free time to spend in the kitchen. While it is true that there are still some more unusual spices and other ingredients that are a little more difficult to source, most of the ingredients you will need can be bought from any decent supermarket. If you are lucky enough to have an Asian supermarket near where you live, you should be able to buy some of the more unusual ingredients there.

While it's always a treat to have a takeaway on a Saturday night, there's nothing more satisfying than creating your own curry and filling the house with the wonderfully fragrant aroma of freshly cooked herbs and spices, so get cooking!

History

These days we take culinary diversity for granted and we're lucky to be able to enjoy food from all over the world, with restaurants and supermarkets catering for every possible cuisine and taste. However, this wasn't always the case, and when exotic spices were first exported around the world from as far back as the Middle Ages, they were seen as rare and valuable commodities, sometimes being traded for prices higher than those fetched for gold. As trade from merchant ships flourished during the eighteenth century, a greater variety of spices became available, but these still would have been the preserve only of the affluent. However, it did mean that Western palates became more attuned to exotic flavours and that these new ingredients gradually found their way on to dinner tables around the world.

With regards to the concept of curry, the word itself has little or no meaning in many of the countries where this style of food is traditionally eaten. While we use it generically to refer to meat, fish or vegetable dishes served in a spicy sauce, so diverse are the cuisines of the Asian countries to which the word relates that it would be impossible to gather them all together under this one term.

It is widely believed that the word 'curry' was originally derived from the Tamil word 'kari', which refers to any type of dish that is eaten as an accompaniment to rice. Over time, the name was adapted to cover the entire cuisine, and dishes were altered to accommodate Western taste buds and the availability of ingredients. Thus the idea of the curry was born, but it is only relatively recently that we have begun to discover the true diversity of our favourite food and been introduced to some more authentic dishes from the many countries providing recipes that come under the 'curry' umbrella.

Basic ingredients

As you begin to work your way through some of the delicious dishes over the following pages you will probably notice that many of the same ingredients pop up in different recipes. This is because the base of many curry recipes is centred on a few key ingredients, with the unique flavour of each dish being built up around this base. Listed here are some of the most-used ingredients.

✻ Chillies

The smaller they are, the hotter the flavour, and many recipes will call for specific types or colours of chilli. This is where much of the heat in curries comes from, but it is the careful blend of chillies with other spices that creates the individual character of each dish.

✻ Coriander

Fragrant, delicate and distinctive, this herb is synonymous with curries and is often used as a garnish.

✻ Cumin

The seeds are often dry-fried first to release their aroma. You will find them in many recipes from across Asia.

✻ Balachaung

A hot Burmese condiment made from deep-fried shallots, garlic, chillies and dried shrimps.

Fennel

As well as being used in main dishes, fennel seeds, which have a subtle aniseed flavour, can also be eaten after a meal to aid digestion.

Garlic

It is no exaggeration to state that you will find garlic listed as an ingredient in most curry recipes. As well as the obvious flavour factor, garlic has many positive health benefits, such as acting as a mild antibiotic and helping to stave off winter colds and flu.

Ginger

This aromatic root has a distinctive flavour and is commonly used in all South and Southeast Asian cuisines. It also has a number of health benefits, the most well known of which is its anti-nausea properties.

Onion

Another ingredient that is found in most curry recipes, onions add texture and flavour to the food. Many recipes start by frying chopped onion, to which a variety of spices are added.

Turmeric

Another fragrant root, turmeric is used to add flavour to dishes but it's the vibrant yellow-orange colour that really makes it such a popular inclusion in so many recipes.

Asafoetida powder

This powder is formed from the sap of the plant. It produces a subtle, oniony flavour when stirred into sauces. Store in an airtight container and use only in small quantities.

Diversity
of curries

When we hear the word 'curry' we
automatically tend to think of
India. However, the cuisines of
countries throughout South and
Southeast Asia all have common
components that make them
curries. The rich use of aromatic
spices and herbs and the heat of
chillies characterize the food of
these countries, but the styles
are still extremely diverse and
distinctive, even between regions.

❋ Bangladesh

Rice is the staple carbohydrate in
Bangladesh, and fish features a great
deal throughout the cuisine of this
country. Many Indian restaurants in
Western countries are actually owned
and run by Bangladeshis, so the chances
are that you are already quite familiar
with some of this food.

❋ India

In a country the size of India it is no
great surprise that there is a huge range
of cookery styles, with different regions
favouring different cooking techniques
and ingredients. Religion also has a
major part to play in food, because
different religions each have their own
rules in relation to diet.

Kerala, in the south-west of the
country, has many thriving fishing
communities and therefore the cuisine is
largely based around fish and rice, with
plenty of hot, spicy flavours. Dishes in
the north of the country take some of
their influence from Persia (modern-day

Iran), dating back to the sixteenth century and the rule of the Moguls, whereas in Tamil Nadu, on the south-western coast, there is a strong vegetarian element to the cookery.

❋ Indonesia

Coconut milk, tamarind, lemon grass and soya – these are just some of the most important ingredients that are widely used in Indonesian cuisine. The country is actually made up of thousands of islands and this unusual geography has a wide-ranging impact on the type of food that people eat.

❋ Malaysia

Rice is also the staple food in Malaysia, although noodles are widely used as well. In fact, there is a great deal of diversity in the cuisine of this country, which is symbolic of the different ethnic groups that make up the population. There are influences from India, Thailand and China and these have all been incorporated into everyday dishes.

❋ Pakistan

Pakistani cuisine takes its influences from its many neighbours and is therefore extremely diverse, varying a great deal between regions. The food tends to become more spicy as you travel further south, but different types of curries can be found all over the country, incorporating both dry and wet sauces.

❋ Thailand

Thai cuisine is a subtle balance of hot, sour and sweet flavours, and the dishes, although sometimes fiery, always have a fresh, light taste to them as well. This is partly due to the inclusion of citrus juice and other fresh ingredients such as lemon grass, that are used widely in Thai dishes.

Basic recipes and techniques

A number of basic recipes and preparation techniques that occur frequently throughout the dishes in this book are included here for easy reference.

✳ Crispy fried onion (Bawang Goreng)

These dried or fresh onions are sprinkled on top of curries and rice dishes in Indonesia. If using dried onion flakes (available from Asian supermarkets), deep-fry 15 g (½ oz) at a time for a few seconds until golden brown. Remove and drain on kitchen paper. For fresh onion, just thinly slice an onion and shallow-fry until crisp and golden. Drain as before.

✳ Spicy aromatic salt

Combine 75 g (3 oz) sea salt with 1 teaspoon each of dry-fried coriander and cumin seeds, and ½ teaspoon each of dry-fried Szechuan pepper, fennel seeds, allspice and sesame seeds. Grind in an electric spice mill or using a pestle and mortar, making it as fine or as coarse as you wish. Store in an airtight jar in a cool, dry place, where it will keep indefinitely.

❋ Cleaning crabs

To prepare the crab meat, remove the legs and claws from the crab and set aside. Remove the undershell and discard the gills. Clean the body of the crab and cut the meat into small chunks. Crack the legs and claws, extract the meat and set aside with the rest of the meat.

❋ Coconut milk – thick and thin

Coconut milk is made by soaking the grated flesh of a coconut in hot water or scalded milk and then straining. It is classified as thick, thin, or coconut cream. Canned coconut milk separates naturally. The top layer can be spooned off for recipes calling for 'cream' and the bottom poured out as 'thin'. Alternatively, you can just shake the can to get the most commonly called-for 'thick' coconut milk.

❋ Green curry paste

Put 7 small green chillies, 2 halved garlic cloves, 1 finely chopped lemon grass stalk (optional), 1 torn lime leaf (optional), 1 chopped shallot, 25 g (1 oz) coriander leaves and stalks, 1 cm (½ inch) piece of peeled and chopped fresh root ginger, 1 teaspoon coriander seeds, ½ teaspoon black peppercorns, ½ teaspoon grated lime rind, ¼ teaspoon salt and 1 tablespoon groundnut oil in a food processor or blender and blend to a thick paste. (Alternatively, put the chillies in a mortar and crush them with a pestle, then add the garlic and crush it into the chillies, and so on with all the other ingredients, finally stirring in the oil with a spoon.) Any leftover paste can be stored in an airtight container in the refrigerator for up to 3 weeks.

✳ Red curry paste

Put 5 large fresh chillies, 1 teaspoon coriander seeds, 2.5 cm (1 inch) piece of peeled and finely chopped galangal, ½ finely chopped lemon grass stalk, 2 halved garlic cloves, ½ roughly chopped shallot, ½ teaspoon lime juice and 1 tablespoons groundnut oil in a food processor or blender and blend to a thick paste. (Alternatively, pound all the ingredients together with a pestle and mortar.) Any leftover paste can be stored in an airtight container in the refridgerator for up to 3 weeks.

✳ Panang curry paste

Put 2 chopped shallots, 4 chopped garlic cloves, 5 deseeded dried chillies, 1½ chopped lemon grass stalks, 1½ coriander roots, 1 cm (½ inch) piece of peeled and chopped root ginger, ¼ teaspoon dry-fried coriander seeds, ½ teaspoon dry-fried cumin seeds, 1 tablespoon crushed roasted peanuts and cashew nuts and 2 tablespoons groundnut oil in a food processor or blender and blend to a smooth paste. (Alternatively, pound all the ingredients together with a pestle and mortar.) Any leftover paste can be stored in an airtight container in the refridgerator for up to 3 weeks.

✳ Mild curry paste

Mix 125 g (4 oz) mild curry powder with 125 ml (4 fl oz) vinegar and enough water to make a paste that is not too runny. Heat 125 ml (4 fl oz) vegetable oil in a large frying pan or wok and add the paste: it will splutter at first but soon settle down. Stir-fry for 15 minutes or so until the water has completely evaporated to leave a creamy paste. If the oil rises to the surface when the paste is set aside, this means it is fully cooked. Transfer the cooled paste to a warm sterilized bottle. Heat a little more oil and pour it on top of the paste to ensure no mould develops. Cover the bottle tightly with a lid. It will keep indefinitely providing all the water had evaporated. Use as required.

✳ Tamarind liquid

Depending on the strength of the liquid required, use either 1 tablespoon tamarind pulp soaked in 150 ml (¼ pint) boiling water or 3 tablespoons tamarind pulp soaked in 250 ml (8 fl oz) boiling water. The latter is obviously a little stronger. Soak the tamarind pulp in the boiling water for 10 minutes, then strain the pulp through a sieve, pressing it against the sieve to extract as much tamarind flavour as possible. Discard the pulp and use the tamarind liquid.

✳ Dhana Jeera

This is a spice mixture made up of ground roasted coriander and cumin. Mix 2 parts coriander to 1 part cumin.

meat

2 tablespoons **vegetable oil**

1 **onion**, chopped

2 **garlic cloves**, crushed

2.5 cm (1 inch) piece of fresh **root ginger**, peeled and finely chopped

1 teaspoon **garam masala**

1 teaspoon **chilli powder**

3 tablespoons **hot curry paste**

1 tablespoon **tomato purée**

500 g (1 lb) lean **minced beef**

1 teaspoon **salt**

175 g (6 oz) **frozen peas**, defrosted

150 ml (¼ pint) **vegetable stock**

3 tablespoons chopped **coriander leaves**

TO GARNISH:

sprigs of **coriander**

Spicy minced beef and pea curry

If you prefer to choose your own cut of meat, ask the butcher to mince if for you.

1 Heat the oil in a heavy-based saucepan, add the chopped onion, garlic, ginger, garam masala and chilli powder and fry over a gentle heat, stirring frequently, for about 5 minutes or until softened.

2 Add the hot curry paste, tomato purée, beef and salt, and mix well so that all the ingredients are evenly coated in the spice mixture. Fry, stirring occasionally, for a further 5 minutes.

3 Stir in the peas and vegetable stock, then cover the pan. Simmer the curry gently for a further 5 minutes. Stir in the chopped coriander and taste, adjusting the salt if necessary. Transfer the curry to a warm serving dish, garnish with sprigs of coriander and serve immediately.

PREP **5** COOK **20** SERVES **4** spicy

Simple beef curry with spinach

If you would like to make this curry hotter, add some of the chilli seeds to it.

1 Heat the ghee or oil in a saucepan, add the onion and garlic and fry over a gentle heat, stirring frequently, for about 5 minutes or until softened but not coloured. Stir in the chillies and fry for a further 2 minutes.

2 Add the cloves, garam masala, coriander, turmeric, chilli powder and cumin. Stir well to mix and fry, stirring constantly, for 2 minutes.

3 Stir in the beef and salt and cook, stirring, for 3 minutes to seal the meat, then add the diced tomatoes, coconut milk and spinach and stir to mix. Cover the pan, then simmer the curry gently, stirring just occasionally, for 20 minutes.

4 Stir in the lemon juice and cook the curry, uncovered, for a further 8–10 minutes, stirring occasionally, until the sauce has thickened. Taste and adjust the seasoning if necessary and serve immediately with the saffron and cardamom rice.

2 tablespoons **ghee** or **vegetable oil**

1 large **onion**, thinly sliced

2 **garlic cloves**, crushed

2 **green chillies**, deseeded and sliced

2 whole **cloves**, bruised

1 teaspoon **garam masala**

1 teaspoon **ground coriander**

1 teaspoon **turmeric**

½ teaspoon **chilli powder**

1½ teaspoons **ground cumin**

625 g (1¼ lb) **fillet of beef**, cut into bite-sized pieces

1 teaspoon **salt**

175 g (6 oz) **tomatoes**, cut into large dice

150 ml (¼ pint) **coconut milk**

250 g (8 oz) ready-washed **young leaf spinach**

1 teaspoon **lemon juice**

TO SERVE:

Saffron and Cardamom Rice (see page 212)

PREP **20**

COOK **40**

SERVES **4**

hot

Beef, pumpkin and pepper curry

5 tablespoons **vegetable oil**

1 **red pepper**, cored, deseeded and cut into chunks

1 **green pepper**, cored, deseeded and cut into chunks

2 **onions**, sliced

1 teaspoon **turmeric**

2 tablespoons **coriander seeds**, lightly crushed

2 teaspoons **caster sugar**

750 g (1½ lb) lean **stewing steak**, cut into small chunks

3 **garlic cloves**, sliced

15 g (½ oz) fresh **root ginger**, peeled and chopped

1 **red chilli**, deseeded and chopped

400 g (13 oz) can chopped **tomatoes**

500 ml (17 fl oz) **beef stock** or **chicken stock**

1 kg (2 lb) **pumpkin**, deseeded

salt

TO SERVE:

crème fraîche

This is a dish that can be prepared in advance, kept in the refrigerator and then reheated when you're ready to eat.

1 Heat the oil in a large heavy-based saucepan. Add the peppers and fry for 4–5 minutes until they start to colour. Lift out with a slotted spoon and set aside. Add the onions, turmeric, coriander, sugar and beef and cook gently for 5 minutes, or until lightly coloured.

2 Add the garlic, ginger and chilli to the pan and cook for 2 minutes, stirring. Add the tomatoes and stock and bring slowly to the boil. Reduce the heat, cover the pan and simmer very gently for 1 hour until the beef is tender.

3 Meanwhile, cut away the skin from the pumpkin and cut the flesh into chunks. Add to the pan with the red and green peppers. Cook gently for 20 minutes until the pumpkin is very soft. Season with salt if necessary and serve with crème fraîche.

PREP
20

COOK
75

SERVES
5–6

rich

Beef and mango curry

This Nepalese recipe combines stewing beef with a mango or brinjal (aubergine) pickle base and fresh mango.

1 Heat the ghee in a large frying pan or wok and stir-fry the curry purée for 5 minutes. Stir in the curry paste and the meat, combining the ingredients well. Continue frying until the meat is sealed – about 5 minutes.

2 Transfer to a heavy lidded casserole and place in a preheated oven, 190°C (375°F), Gas Mark 5, for 20 minutes.

3 Meanwhile, scoop all the flesh from the mango. Place it in a blender or food processor and work to a purée. Add it to the casserole with the chopped pickle, coriander and salt to taste, with a little water to moisten if necessary.

4 Return the casserole to the oven and cook for a further 25 minutes. At the end of the cooking time, spoon off any excess oil before serving. Garnish with fresh mango slices and sprigs of parsley.

4 tablespoons **ghee**

1 quantity **curry purée** (see page 24)

1 tablespoon **mild curry paste** (see page 17)

750 g (1½ lb) **stewing beef**, cubed

1 **mango**

3 tablespoons **mild mango pickle** or **brinjal pickle**, finely chopped

1 tablespoon chopped **coriander leaves**

salt

TO GARNISH:
fresh **mango** slices
sprigs of **parsley**

PREP
10

COOK
55

SERVES
4

fruity

4 tablespoons **ghee**

2 tablespoons **mild curry paste** (see page 17)

750 g (1½ lb) **stewing beef**, cubed

4 **tomatoes**, chopped

4 tablespoons **dried fenugreek leaves**

1 tablespoon **garam masala**

salt

CURRY PURÉE:

6 tablespoons **ghee**

2–4 **garlic cloves**, finely chopped

5 cm (2 inch) piece of fresh **root ginger**, peeled and finely chopped

½ **onion**, finely chopped

2 teaspoons **mild curry paste** (see page 17)

1 teaspoon **tomato purée**

1 tablespoon chopped **coriander leaves**

TO GARNISH:

2 tablespoons chopped **parsley**

Beef with fenugreek

Cubes of beef are cooked with dried fenugreek leaves, called 'methi', to produce this moist savoury curry. Fenugreek leaves are widely used, either fresh or dried, in Indian cooking.

1 To make the curry purée, heat the 6 tablespoons of ghee in a large frying pan or wok. Stir-fry the garlic for 1 minute. Add the ginger and stir-fry for 1 minute more. Add the onion and stir-fry for 2–3 minutes more. Stir in the 2 teaspoons of curry paste, tomato purée and coriander with enough water to prevent the mixture from sticking. Simmer for 5 minutes.

2 Heat the 4 tablespoons of ghee in another large frying pan or wok and stir-fry the curry purée for 5 minutes. Stir the 2 tablespoons of curry paste in well to blend and add the cubes of beef. Stir-fry for about 5 minutes more to seal the meat.

3 Transfer the meat and sauce to a heavy lidded casserole and bake in a preheated oven, 190°C (375°F), Gas Mark 5, for 20 minutes. Stir in the tomatoes, dried fenugreek, garam masala and salt to taste, with a little water to moisten if necessary. Continue cooking for a further 25 minutes. If, at the end of the cooking time, there is an excess of oil, spoon it off before serving. Garnish with chopped parsley.

PREP **15**

COOK **70**

SERVES **4**

mild

Spicy beef curry

This dish of marinated beef cooked with milk, almonds and coconut uses a curry paste, which is simply a 'wet' blend of spices – as opposed to a 'dry' blend such as garam masala – cooked with oil and vinegar, which help to preserve them.

1 Beat the beef steaks with a rolling pin or the back of a wooden spoon until they are 5 mm (¼ inch) thick. Cut each steak in half to give 8 pieces. Place the steaks in a non-metallic dish. Add the red wine and spices and leave to marinate in the refrigerator for up to 24 hours.

2 Heat the oil in a frying pan or wok and stir-fry the curry purée for 5 minutes. Add the curry paste and mix well. Lift the steaks out of the marinade and add to the pan 2 at a time. Fry the steaks quickly to seal – allowing about 20 seconds on each side.

3 When all the steaks are in the pan and are brown, add the milk, ground almonds, coconut and the marinade. Simmer for 10 minutes, until the meat is cooked.

4 Transfer to a warmed serving dish and pour the cream over the top. Garnish with parsley and pistachio nuts.

750 g (1½ lb) lean **beef rump, fillet** or **topside**, sliced into 4 steaks

150 ml (¼ pint) **red wine**

2 teaspoons **garam masala**

1 teaspoon **ground mace**

½ teaspoon **ground cinnamon**

4 tablespoons **vegetable oil**

1 quantity **curry purée** (see page 24)

1 tablespoon **mild curry paste** (see page 17)

175 ml (6 fl oz) **milk**

2 tablespoons **ground almonds**

2 tablespoons **desiccated coconut**

4 tablespoons **double cream**

salt

TO GARNISH:

sprigs of **parsley**

chopped **pistachio nuts**

PREP **20***

COOK **20**

SERVES **4**

creamy

* plus up to 24 hours marinating

Beef kofta curry

625 g (1¼ lb) lean **minced beef**

1 teaspoon peeled and finely grated fresh **root ginger**

2 teaspoons **fennel seeds**, roughly crushed using a pestle and mortar

1 teaspoon **ground cinnamon**

1 teaspoon **turmeric**

2 tablespoons **mild curry powder**

500 ml (17 fl oz) **tomato passata**

salt and **pepper**

TO GARNISH:

natural yogurt

mint leaves

TO SERVE:

chapattis or **flatbreads**

salad

Small, spicy balls of minced beef cooked in a smooth, spicy sauce make a warming supper. Serve with Indian flatbreads and a fresh Indian salad or salsa. Wrap the koftas and salad up in the bread for an informal meal.

1 Place the mince and ginger in a large mixing bowl. Add the fennel seeds to the mixture with the cinnamon, season and, using your hands, mix thoroughly. Form the mixture into small, walnut-sized balls and set aside.

2 Place the turmeric, curry powder and passata in a wide, nonstick saucepan and bring to the boil. Season, reduce the heat and carefully place the meatballs in the sauce. Cover and cook gently for 15–20 minutes, stirring and turning the meatballs around occasionally, until they are cooked through.

3 Remove from the heat, drizzle with the yogurt and scatter with the mint leaves. Serve with chapattis or other flatbreads and salad.

PREP **10**　COOK **20**　SERVES **4**　spicy

Burmese beef and peanut curry

This dish from the Shan state of north-east Burma is often accompanied by bean soup, fish curry, fried peanuts and Coconut Rice (see page 217) and is traditionally assembled in a large lacquerware bowl.

1 Mix the salt, flour and turmeric together and sprinkle over the beef cubes in a bowl. Heat the oil in a large heavy-based frying pan and fry the onions until softened.

2 Add the garlic, paprika, coriander, garam masala, ginger and lemon grass and cook for 3–4 minutes or until the onion has browned. Remove from the pan. Add the beef, a few pieces at a time, and brown on all sides.

3 Return the onions and spices to the pan. Add the coconut, with the soaking water if applicable, the measured water and the tomatoes. Cover and simmer very gently for 1½–2 hours until the sauce has reduced and become thick and the meat is tender. Season to taste with salt and pepper. Serve sprinkled with peanuts and the balachaung.

1 teaspoon **salt**

1 tablespoon **plain flour**

2 teaspoons **turmeric**

1 kg (2 lb) **braising beef**, cubed

4 tablespoons **vegetable oil**

3 **onions**, finely chopped

4 **garlic cloves**, crushed

1 teaspoon **paprika**

1 tablespoon **ground coriander**

2 tablespoons **garam masala**

7.5 cm (3 inch) piece of fresh **root ginger**, peeled and finely chopped

1 **lemon grass stalk**, finely chopped

flesh from 1 **coconut**, grated, or 50 g (2 oz) **desiccated coconut**, soaked in warm water for 30 minutes

900 ml (1½ pints) **water**

4 **tomatoes**, quartered

salt and **pepper**

TO SERVE:

3 tablespoons **roasted peanuts**, chopped

2 tablespoons **balachaung** (see page 10)

PREP
30

COOK
120

SERVES
4–6

citrus

3 tablespoons **vegetable oil**

4 **shallots**, finely chopped

3 large **garlic cloves**, crushed

500 g (1 lb) **sirloin beef**, sliced

150 ml (¼ pint) **tamarind liquid** (see page 17)

4 **kaffir lime leaves**, shredded

1 teaspoon **shrimp paste**

300 ml (½ pint) **coconut milk**

150 ml (¼ pint) **beef stock** or **water**

1 teaspoon **caster sugar**

1–2 tablespoons **fish sauce**, to taste

125 g (4 oz) **pea aubergines** or larger **green aubergines**, quartered

1 large **red chilli**, deseeded and finely chopped

juice of 1 **lime**

10–15 **sweet basil leaves**

SPICE PASTE:

3 **red bird chillies**, chopped

1 **lemon grass stalk**, chopped

5 cm (2 inch) piece of fresh **galangal**, peeled and sliced

3 **coriander roots**, finely chopped

Aubergine, beef and tamarind curry

Cambodian cuisine contains elements from the cooking of the countries that surround it – Thailand, Vietnam and Laos. This beef curry uses tart tamarind, scented lemon grass, pungent fish sauce and hot bird chillies.

1 Place the spice paste ingredients in a blender or food processor and blend to a smooth paste.

2 Heat the oil in a saucepan and fry the shallots and garlic for 2–3 minutes. Add the spice paste and fry for a further 2–3 minutes.

3 Add the beef to the pan and sear on all sides. Add the tamarind liquid, kaffir lime leaves, shrimp paste, coconut milk, stock, sugar and fish sauce. Simmer for 20 minutes.

4 Add the aubergines to the pan with the chopped red chilli, lime juice and basil leaves and simmer for 5 minutes.

PREP **25**

COOK **30**

SERVES **4**

hot

Beef rendang

Hot, spicy and dry, a rendang's flavour improves with long slow cooking, as well as being kept for a couple of days in the refrigerator.

1 Put the spice paste ingredients up to and including the chillies in a blender or food processor and process until roughly chopped or pound in a mortar with a pestle. Add the lemon grass and onions and process to a dry paste. Add the tamarind liquid and blend to a soft paste.

2 Heat the oil in a large saucepan and fry the beef until browned on all sides. Remove with a slotted spoon and reserve.

3 Add the spice paste to the hot pan and fry for 2–3 minutes, stirring constantly. Return the beef to the pan with all the remaining ingredients and bring slowly to the boil, stirring constantly.

4 Reduce the heat and simmer very gently for 4–4½ hours, stirring occasionally, until the meat is tender and the sauce has reduced and thickened.

5 When the sauce is very thick, increase the heat and, stirring constantly, fry the beef in the thick sauce until the meat is a rich brown colour.

PREP **30** COOK **270** SERVES **4–6** spicy

3 tablespoons **coconut** or **vegetable oil**

750 g (1½ lb) **braising beef**, sliced

900 ml (1½ pints) **coconut milk**

150 ml (¼ pint) **water**

1 tablespoon **palm sugar** or **soft brown sugar**

4 **kaffir lime leaves**, shredded

3 **star anise**

1 large **cinnamon stick**

½ teaspoon **salt**

SPICE PASTE:

1 teaspoon **salt**

1 teaspoon **turmeric**

½ teaspoon **chilli powder**

6 **garlic cloves**, chopped

5 cm (2 inch) piece of fresh **root ginger**, peeled and grated

5 cm (2 inch) piece of fresh **galangal**, peeled and grated

1 teaspoon **black peppercorns**, crushed

4 **cardamom pods**, bruised

4 **red chillies**, chopped

1 **lemon grass stalk**, chopped

3 large **onions**, chopped

2 tablespoons **tamarind liquid** (see page 17)

1 tablespoon **vegetable oil**

1½ tablespoons **Panang curry paste** (see page 16)

6 tablespoons **coconut milk**

3 **lime leaves**, finely shredded, plus 2, torn, to garnish

125 g (4 oz) **beef topside**, cut into bite-sized pieces

3 tablespoons **chicken stock**

1 large **red chilli**, sliced on the diagonal

3 tablespoons **palm sugar** or **soft brown sugar**

50 g (2 oz) **peas**

Panang beef curry

If you eat out at Thai restaurants, you have probably seen this on the menu. You can substitute the beef for chicken or pork, if you like.

1 Heat the oil in a wok, add the curry paste and cook for 30 seconds. Pour in the coconut milk, add the lime leaves and stir and cook for 1 minute.

2 Add the beef, stock, chilli and sugar and increase the heat and cook, stirring, for 1 minute, then reduce the heat and simmer for 7 minutes.

3 Add the peas and simmer for 3 more minutes. The sauce should thicken considerably but add a little more stock if it seems to be getting too dry. Serve garnished with lime leaves.

PREP
5

COOK
15

SERVES
2

quick

Thai green beef curry

This is another classic Thai dish made with green curry paste and coconut milk. Again, the beef can be substituted for chicken as an alternative.

1 Heat the oil in a wok. Add the ginger and shallots and stir-fry over a low heat for about 3 minutes or until softened. Add the green curry paste and fry for 2 minutes.

2 Add the beef to the wok, stir until evenly coated in the spice mixture and fry for 3 minutes to seal the meat. Stir in the coconut milk and bring to the boil. Reduce the heat and cook the curry over a low heat, stirring occasionally, for about 10 minutes or until the beef is cooked through and the sauce has thickened.

3 Stir in the fish sauce, sugar, lime leaves, tamarind liquid and chilli. Cook the curry for a further 5 minutes, then season to taste.

4 Serve the curry hot, garnished with yellow pepper strips and fried garlic and topped with a red chilli curl, if liked.

2 tablespoons **groundnut oil**

2.5 cm (1 inch) piece of fresh **root ginger**, peeled and finely chopped

2 **shallots**, chopped

4 tablespoons **green curry paste** (see page 15)

500 g (1 lb) **fillet of beef**, cubed

300 ml (½ pint) **coconut milk**

4 tablespoons **fish sauce**

1 teaspoon **palm sugar** or **soft brown sugar**

3 **kaffir lime leaves**, finely chopped, or ¼ teaspoon grated **lime rind**

2 teaspoons **tamarind liquid** (see page 17)

1 **green chilli**, deseeded and finely sliced

salt and **pepper**

TO GARNISH:

yellow pepper strips

fried chopped **garlic**

red chilli strip, curled (optional)

PREP
10

COOK
25

SERVES
4

creamy

3 tablespoons **groundnut oil**

3 tablespoons **red curry paste** (see page 16)

½ teaspoon **ground coriander**

½ teaspoon **ground cumin**

4 **kaffir lime leaves**, shredded

500 g (1 lb) **fillet of beef**, cut into thin strips

400 ml (14 fl oz) can **coconut milk**

2 tablespoons **crunchy peanut butter**

2 teaspoons **fish sauce**

1 tablespoon **palm sugar** or **soft brown sugar**

TO GARNISH:

sprigs of **coriander** (optional)

Thai red beef curry

This recipe uses red curry paste to give it a distinctive colour and flavour. Both red and green curry pastes contain plenty of chillies and lemon grass, resulting in a hot but fresh flavour.

1 Heat the oil in a heavy-based saucepan. Add the curry paste, coriander, cumin and lime leaves. Cook over a low heat, stirring frequently, for 3 minutes.

2 Add the beef strips to the pan, stir to coat them evenly in the curry paste and cook gently, stirring frequently, for 5 minutes.

3 Add half of the coconut milk to the pan, stir to combine and simmer gently for 4 minutes until most of the coconut milk has been absorbed.

4 Stir in the remaining coconut milk with the peanut butter, fish sauce and sugar. Simmer gently for 5 minutes until the sauce is thick and the beef is tender. Garnish with coriander sprigs, if using, and serve immediately.

PREP **10**

COOK **20**

SERVES **4**

hot

Malaysian beef and potato curry

This hearty curry makes the most of fragrant spices to deliver an intricate flavour. The beef and potatoes act as sponges for the delicious paste.

1 To make the spice paste, heat the oil in a saucepan, add the shallots, garlic and ginger, and fry over a low heat, stirring frequently, for 5 minutes until softened. And the remaining ingredients and fry for 1 minute.

2 Add the beef and stir well to coat it in the spice mixture. Add the potatoes, chillies, salt and coconut milk. Stir to combine, bring to the boil, then reduce the heat, cover the pan and simmer gently, stirring occasionally, for 40 minutes until the beef strips are tender and the potatoes are cooked.

3 Stir in the lime juice and sugar and cook, uncovered, for a further 2 minutes. Taste and adjust the seasoning, if necessary, and serve hot, garnished with sliced red chillies.

PREP **20**

COOK **50**

SERVES **4**

hot

375 g (12 oz) **sirloin steak**, cut into 1 cm (½ inch) strips

300 g (10 oz) **potatoes**, peeled and cut into chunks

2 large **red chillies**, deseeded and finely chopped

½ teaspoon **salt**

300 ml (½ pint) **coconut milk**

2 tablespoons **lime juice**

1 teaspoon **palm sugar** or **soft brown sugar**

SPICE PASTE:

2 tablespoons **groundnut oil**

5 **shallots**, chopped

2 **garlic cloves**, crushed

5 cm (2 inch) piece of fresh **root ginger**, peeled and grated

2 tablespoons hot **curry powder**

1 teaspoon **ground cinnamon**

1 teaspoon **ground cumin**

1 teaspoon **ground coriander**

¼ teaspoon **ground cardamom**

4 **curry leaves**

1 **star anise**

4 **cloves**

TO GARNISH:

red chillies, sliced

meat 33

2 tablespoons **groundnut oil**

500 g (1 lb) **lean beef**, thinly sliced

400 ml (14 fl oz) can **coconut milk**

salt and **pepper**

SPICE PASTE:

2 tablespoons **yellow bean sauce**

3 tablespoons **red curry paste** (see page 16)

2 tablespoons **palm sugar** or **soft brown sugar**

4 **shallots**, chopped

2 **garlic cloves**, chopped

2 large **red chillies**, deseeded and chopped

1 **lemon grass stalk**, chopped, or ¼ teaspoon grated **lemon rind**

2.5 cm (1 inch) piece of fresh **galangal** or fresh **root ginger**, peeled and chopped

½ teaspoon **shrimp paste**

4 tablespoons **lime juice**

TO GARNISH:

½ **red pepper**, cut into thin strips

2 **spring onions**, shredded

Chiang Mai jungle curry with beef

The fiery flavours of this curry are typical of northern Thailand. Although this version uses beef, jungle dishes from northern Thailand often contain more exotic meats such as monkey or even snake!

1 Place the spice paste ingredients in a blender or food processor and blend to a smooth paste. Alternatively, pound using a pestle and mortar.

2 Heat the oil in a large flameproof casserole, add the beef and stir-fry over a moderate heat for 3 minutes to seal the meat. Stir in the paste and stir-fry for a further 3 minutes. Pour the coconut milk into the casserole, stir to mix and bring to the boil. Reduce the heat, cover the casserole dish and simmer the curry gently, stirring occasionally, for 50 minutes or until the beef is tender. Season to taste.

3 Garnish the curry with strips of red pepper and spring onions.

PREP
15

COOK
60

SERVES
3

fiery

Calcutta beef curry

This rich and hearty curry consists of beef simmered for a long time in a mixture of milk and spices until the meat is tender and the sauce reduced.

1 Put the spice mixture ingredients into a large bowl. Mix in a little of the milk to make a paste, then gradually stir in the remaining milk. Add the cubes of beef and stir well until the beef is evenly coated.

2 Melt the ghee in a heavy-based frying pan or wok, add the onions, garlic and ginger and fry gently for 4–5 minutes, until soft.

3 Remove the beef from the milk and spice mixture with a slotted spoon, add to the pan and stir-fry over a moderate heat until browned on all sides.

4 Increase the heat, add the milk and spice mixture and bring to the boil. Cover the pan, lower the heat and cook gently for 1½–2 hours, or until the beef is tender and the sauce reduced.

5 Just before serving, sprinkle in the garam masala. Increase the heat and boil off any excess liquid to leave a thick sauce. Transfer the curry to a warmed serving dish and serve immediately.

PREP **15** COOK **120** SERVES **4–6** **rich**

1 litre (1¾ pints) **milk**

1–1.25 kg (2–2½ lb) **braising steak**, trimmed and cut into 4 cm (1¾ inch) cubes

50 g (2 oz) **ghee**

2 large **onions**, thinly sliced

5 **garlic cloves**, thinly sliced

7.5 cm (3 inch) piece of fresh **root ginger**, peeled and thinly sliced

2 teaspoons **garam masala**

SPICE MIXTURE:

1 teaspoon **salt**

1 tablespoon **chilli powder**

2 teaspoons **ground coriander**

1 teaspoon **pepper**

1½ teaspoons **turmeric**

1 teaspoon **ground cumin**

2 tablespoons **ghee**

1 large **onion**, thinly sliced

3 **garlic cloves**, crushed

2.5 cm (1 inch) piece of fresh **root ginger**, peeled and finely chopped

2 tablespoons **Sri Lankan spice mixture** (see page 111)

1 teaspoon **turmeric**

1 tablespoon **mustard seeds**

1 teaspoon **salt**

1 tablespoon **white wine vinegar**

2 **red chillies**, deseeded and thinly sliced

4 **tomatoes** (approximate weight 275 g (9 oz), chopped

625 g (1¼ lb) **fillet of beef**, cut into 5 cm (2 inch) cubes

1 teaspoon **palm sugar** or **soft brown sugar**

TO SERVE:

Sri Lankan Yellow Rice (see page 218)

Ceylon beef curry

This delicious dish from Sri Lanka is very quick to prepare. You should be able to find ghee in most large supermarkets.

1 Heat the ghee in a heavy-based saucepan, add the onion, garlic and ginger, and fry over a low heat, stirring frequently, for 5 minutes until softened.

2 Add the spice mixture, turmeric and mustard seeds and fry over a low heat, stirring constantly, for a further 2 minutes until aromatic.

3 Stir in the salt, vinegar, chillies, tomatoes and beef and mix well to coat the beef evenly in the spices.

4 Cover the pan and cook the curry over a low heat, stirring occasionally, for 50 minutes or until the meat is very tender.

5 Remove the lid, stir in the sugar and cook the curry uncovered for a further 10 minutes, stirring occasionally, until the sauce is thick. Taste and adjust the seasoning if necessary and serve immediately with the Sri Lankan rice.

PREP **15**

COOK **75**

SERVES **4**

spicy

Burmese beef and pumpkin curry

Pumpkin works surprisingly well in curry dishes as its distinctive flavour is not lost amongst the spices. It also holds its shape although you need to be careful not to let it overcook or it will become mushy.

1 Place the spice paste ingredients in a blender or food processor and blend to a coarse paste. Heat the oil in a large flameproof casserole, add the spice paste and fry over a gentle heat, stirring for about 5 minutes or until softened. Add the chilli flakes and turmeric and fry for a further 2 minutes.

2 Add the beef to the pan, stir well to coat the beef in the spice mixture and fry, stirring frequently, for 5 minutes. Add the stock and sugar to the pan and bring to the boil. Reduce the heat, cover the pan and cook the curry, stirring occasionally, for 35 minutes or until the beef is tender.

3 Add the pumpkin and salt to the pan, stir gently to mix, cover and cook for a further 10 minutes or until the pumpkin is tender. Taste and adjust the seasoning, if necessary. Serve the curry garnished with ginger, if liked.

3 tablespoons **sesame oil**

2 teaspoons **dried chilli flakes**

1 teaspoon **turmeric**

625 g (1¼ lb) **sirloin steak**, cut into 2.5 cm (1 inch) cubes

300 ml (½ pint) **beef stock**

1 teaspoon **palm sugar** or **soft brown sugar**

500 g (1 lb) **pumpkin**, peeled, deseeded and cut into 2.5 cm (1 inch) cubes

½ teaspoon **salt**

1.5 cm (¾ inch) piece of fresh **root ginger**, peeled and finely shredded, to garnish (optional)

SPICE PASTE:

2 large **onions**, chopped

4 **garlic cloves**, chopped

2 stalks of **lemon grass**, chopped

2.5 cm (1 inch) piece of fresh **root ginger**, chopped

TO GARNISH:

fresh chopped **ginger**

PREP **25**

COOK **50**

SERVES **4–6**

hot

Meatball curry

500 g (1 lb) **minced beef**

2 large **onions**, chopped

4 **garlic cloves**, crushed

2 teaspoons **turmeric**

2 teaspoons **chilli powder**

2 teaspoons **ground coriander**

1½ teaspoons **ground cumin**

1 teaspoon **ground ginger**

2 teaspoons **salt**

1 **egg**, beaten

vegetable oil, for deep-frying

125 g (4 oz) **ghee** or 2 tablespoons **vegetable oil**

200 ml (7 fl oz) **water**

TO GARNISH:

mint or **coriander leaves**

If you are preparing this for a dinner party, make the meatballs in advance and keep them covered in the refridgerator until you are ready to cook.

1 Put the minced beef in a bowl with half of the onions, garlic, spices and salt. Stir well and then bind the mixture together with the beaten egg.

2 Divide the minced beef mixture into 12 equal portions and, using your hands, shape each one into a small ball.

3 Heat the oil in a heavy-based saucepan until it is very hot. Add the meatballs in batches and deep-fry for 5 minutes. Remove and drain on absorbent kitchen paper and then set aside.

4 Heat the ghee or vegetable oil in a large saucepan, add the remaining onions and garlic and fry gently for 4–5 minutes until soft. Add the remaining spices and salt and fry for 3 minutes, stirring constantly.

5 Add the meatballs and coat them in the spices. Add the measured water and bring to the boil. Lower the heat and simmer gently for 30 minutes. Serve garnished with mint or coriander leaves.

PREP **30**   COOK **40**   SERVES **4**   spicy

Beef and new potato curry

This is a really great way to make the most of seasonal new potatoes. Make sure they are really small and all of a similar shape and size so they are cooked at the same time.

1 Heat the oil in a large pan, add the onions and fry until lightly browned. Add the garlic, chilli powder, cumin, ground coriander and ginger and cook gently for 5 minutes, stirring occasionally. If the mixture becomes dry, add 2 tablespoons of water.

2 Add the cubes of beef and cook, stirring, until browned all over. Add the tomato purée, salt to taste and just enough water to cover the meat, then stir very well. Bring to the boil, cover and simmer for about 1 hour, or until the meat is almost tender. Add the potatoes and whole chillies and simmer until the potatoes are cooked.

4 tablespoons **vegetable oil**

2 **onions**, finely chopped

2 **garlic cloves**, chopped

1 teaspoon **chilli powder**

1 tablespoon **ground cumin**

1½ tablespoons **ground coriander**

2.5 cm (1 inch) piece of fresh **root ginger**, peeled and finely chopped

750 g (1½ lb) **stewing steak**, cubed

2 tablespoons **tomato purée**

375 g (12 oz) small **new potatoes**

4 **green chillies**

salt

PREP 15

COOK 90

SERVES 4

hot

50 g (2 oz) **red lentils**

50 g (2 oz) **split yellow lentils** (moong dhal)

50 g (2 oz) **chickpeas**

750 g (1½ lb) **lamb fillet**, cut into 5 cm (2 inch) cubes

300 g (10 oz) **aubergine**, cubed

250 g (8 oz) **pumpkin**, peeled, deseeded and cubed

125 g (4 oz) **potato**, cubed

2 **onions**, roughly chopped

2 **tomatoes**, skinned and chopped

75 g (3 oz) **spinach**

3 tablespoons **ghee** or **vegetable oil**

1 large **onion**, thinly sliced

masala sauce (see page 44)

dry spice mixture (see page 45)

2 tablespoons **tomato purée**

salt and **pepper**

TO GARNISH:

crispy fried onions (see page 14)

Lamb dhansak

A hearty dish of lamb and lentils, this is a filling meal that can be served with bread instead of rice, if you prefer.

1 Soak both lots of lentils and the chickpeas overnight in separate bowls of cold water.

2 The next day, drain the pulses and place them in a large saucepan with the lamb. Pour over enough boiling water to cover the lentils and meat and season generously with salt. Bring to the boil, skim any scum from the surface, then cover and simmer, stirring occasionally, for about 20 minutes.

3 Tip all the prepared vegetables (except the sliced onion) into the pan, stir and continue cooking for a further 40 minutes until the lentils and vegetables are cooked and the lamb is tender. Drain the liquid from the pan and reserve. Remove the pieces of meat with a slotted spoon. Set the meat aside and tip the vegetables and lentils into a blender or food processor. Process to a thick purée.

PREP **30***

COOK **105**

SERVES **6**

hearty

* plus overnight soaking

4 Heat the ghee or oil in a large heavy-based sauté pan and fry the sliced onion over a low heat for 5 minutes until it is softened and golden.

5 Add the masala sauce to the softened onion and cook gently for a further 3 minutes. Stir in the dry spice mixture and cook, stirring, for 3 minutes.

6 Add the lamb and vegetable purée to the pan, together with the tomato purée and reserved cooking liquid. Season, cover and simmer for 30 minutes until thick. If it becomes too dry, add a little water. Taste and adjust the seasoning if necessary. Transfer to a warmed serving dish, garnish with fried onions and serve.

Lamb balti

625 g (1¼ lb) lean **lamb fillet** or **leg**

1 tablespoon peeled and freshly minced **root ginger**

2 **garlic cloves**, crushed

150 ml (¼ pint) **natural yogurt**

12 **cardamom pods**

2 tablespoons **sunflower** or **vegetable oil**

2 large **onions**, cut into wedges

1 **cinnamon stick**, halved

1 teaspoon **turmeric**

1 teaspoon **cumin seeds**

2 **bay leaves**

2 teaspoons **medium curry paste**

250 g (8 oz) can **chopped tomatoes**

450 ml (¾ pint) **lamb** or **chicken stock**

625 g (1¼ lb) **potatoes**, peeled and cut into small chunks

3 tablespoons chopped **coriander leaves**

salt and **pepper**

TO SERVE:

nann bread or **rice**

poppadums

This quick version of a balti uses curry paste with some whole spices to intensify and freshen the flavour. It's very easy to assemble if you have a good variety of spices in your storecupboard.

1 Cut the lamb into small chunks, discarding any fat. Put the lamb, ginger, garlic and yogurt in a heavy-based frying pan and heat until bubbling. Reduce the heat, cover the pan and simmer gently for 20 minutes.

2 Meanwhile, open the cardamom pods by gently pounding them with the end of a rolling pin to expose the seeds. Heat the oil in a saucepan, add the cardamoms, onions, cinnamon, turmeric, cumin and bay leaves and fry gently for 5 minutes.

3 Add the lamb mixture, curry paste, tomatoes and stock and bring to a simmer. Cover and cook for 15 minutes until the lamb is tender and the sauce has thickened slightly.

4 Add the potatoes to the pan and cook, covered, for a further 15 minutes until they are tender. Stir in the chopped coriander and serve with nann bread or rice and poppadums.

PREP **25**   COOK **60**   SERVES **4**   spicy

Lamb korma

This favourite mild lamb curry is cooked with yogurt, coconut milk, saffron, ginger and ground almonds. Serve with cold beer for a perfect summer supper.

1 Put the lamb in a non-metallic bowl. Mix together the yogurt, saffron and its water and the salt. Pour over the lamb, cover and leave to marinate for 2 hours.

2 Place the curry paste ingredients in a blender or food processor and blend to a smooth paste.

3 Heat the ghee in a frying pan, add the cardamom, cinnamon and cumin and fry over a low heat for 1 minute. Stir in the curry paste and cook, stirring frequently, for another 5 minutes.

4 Add the coconut milk and the lamb and saffron yogurt, bring to the boil, then turn down the heat. Cover and cook very gently, stirring occasionally, for 45 minutes, or until the lamb is tender and the sauce is thick.

5 Stir in 2 tablespoons of the coriander leaves and serve with the rest of the coriander scattered over the top.

750 g (1½ lb) boneless **leg of lamb**, cut into cubes

150 ml (¼ pint) **natural yogurt**

½ teaspoon **saffron threads**, soaked in 2 tablespoons boiling **water** for 10 minutes

1 teaspoon **salt**

2 tablespoons **ghee**

¼ teaspoon **ground cardamom**

½ teaspoon **cinnamon**

1½ teaspoons **ground cumin**

300 ml (½ pint) **coconut milk**

3 tablespoons chopped **coriander leaves**

CURRY PASTE:

2 **onions**, finely chopped

3 **garlic cloves**, chopped

2.5 cm (1 inch) piece of fresh **root ginger**, peeled and chopped

2 **green chillies**, deseeded and chopped

50 g (2 oz) **ground almonds**

150 ml (¼ pint) **water**

PREP
25

COOK
50

SERVES
4

creamy

* plus 2 hours marinating

750 g (1½ lb) lean **lamb**, cubed

1 quantity **tandoori marinade** (see page 117)

MASALA SAUCE:

4 tablespoons **ghee**

1 quantity **curry purée** (see page 24)

1 tablespoon **tandoori paste**

2 teaspoons **tomato purée**

2 **tomatoes**, skinned and chopped

1 **red pepper**, cored, deseeded and puréed

1 tablespoon chopped **coriander leaves**

1 tablespoon **ground almonds**

2 tablespoons **single cream**

sugar, to taste

salt

TO GARNISH:

lime slices

sprigs of **parsley**

Lamb tikka masala

Cubes of lamb are marinated in a tandoori marinade, then cooked on skewers and added to a masala sauce.

1 Combine the lamb and tandoori marinade in a non-metallic bowl. Cover and leave in the refrigerator for about 24 hours.

2 Remove the pieces of lamb from the marinade, reserving the marinade. Thread the pieces of lamb on to 4 metal or presoaked wooden skewers and cook under a preheated moderate grill for 15–20 minutes, turning them once halfway through the cooking time.

3 Meanwhile, make the masala sauce. Heat the ghee in a large frying pan or wok. Add the curry purée and stir-fry for 5 minutes. Add the tandoori paste and the reserved marinade and stir-fry for 2 minutes. Add the tomato purée, chopped tomatoes and puréed red pepper. Bring to simmering point and add a little water, if necessary, to achieve a creamy textured sauce. Add the coriander, ground almonds, cream and sugar and salt to taste.

4 When the lamb tikkas are cooked, remove them from the skewers and stir them into the masala sauce. Serve garnished with lime slices and parsley.

PREP
30*

COOK
30

SERVES
4

mild

* plus 24 hours marinating

Goan lamb and pork curry

In this unusual curry from Goa, two different types of meat are cooked together.

1 Heat the oil in a heavy-based pan, add the onions, garlic, ginger and chillies and cook over a low heat, stirring frequently, for about 5 minutes, until softened.

2 Place the spice mixture ingredients in an electric spice mill or use a pestle and mortar and grind to produce a fine powder. Add the ground spices to the pan and fry for a further 1 minute.

3 Add the pieces of lamb and pork to the pan, together with the salt. Coat the meat in the spices and cook for 2 minutes. Add the measured water and the vinegar to the pan and stir well to combine the ingredients. Cover and simmer over a gentle heat, stirring occasionally, for about 45 minutes, or until the meat is tender.

4 Remove the lid, increase the heat and cook for a further 15 minutes, stirring frequently, until the sauce is thick and dark. Taste and adjust the seasoning if necessary.

5 Transfer the curry to a warmed serving dish and garnish with chilli rings. Serve with the saffron and cardamom rice.

PREP **20**

COOK **70**

SERVES **6**

meaty

3 tablespoons **vegetable oil**

2 **onions**, finely chopped

3 **garlic cloves**, crushed

1 tablespoon peeled and grated fresh **root ginger**

2 large **red chillies**, quartered lengthways and deseeded

375 g (12 oz) **lamb fillet**, cut into bite-sized pieces

375 g (12 oz) lean **pork**, cut into bite-sized pieces

1 teaspoon **salt**

150 ml (¼ pint) **water**

75 ml (3 fl oz) **malt vinegar**

TO GARNISH:

1 **green** and 1 **red chilli**, cut into rings

TO SERVE:

Saffron and Cardamom Rice (see page 212)

DRY SPICE MIXTURE:

1 teaspoon **ground cumin**

1 teaspoon **ground coriander**

1 teaspoon **chilli powder**

1 tablespoon **black mustard seeds**

1 tablespoon **black onion seeds**

1 tablespoon **garam masala**

500 g (1 lb) lean **minced lamb**

1 tablespoon peeled and grated fresh **root ginger**

1 large **red chilli**, deseeded and very finely chopped

2 tablespoons chopped **coriander leaves**

1 tablespoon **garam masala**

1½ teaspoons **salt**

¼ teaspoon **pepper**

3 tablespoons **vegetable oil**

150 ml (¼ pint) **natural yogurt**

1 teaspoon **palm sugar** or **soft brown sugar**

½ teaspoon **chilli powder**

300 ml (½ pint) **water**

TO GARNISH:

pinch of **ground cardamom**

sprigs of **coriander**

TO SERVE:

nanns or **parathas**

Kashmiri kofta curry

A fragrant meatball curry that has a creamy flavour and just a hint of heat. You can make the meatballs in advance to save time.

1 To make the lamb meatballs, place the lamb, ginger, red chilli, coriander, 1 teaspoon of the garam masala, 1 teaspoon of the salt and the pepper in a bowl. Mix thoroughly, then divide the mixture into 16 and shape each portion into a small meatball.

2 Heat the oil in a heavy-based frying pan, add the meatballs and fry over a gentle heat for 5 minutes, turning occasionally, to seal them. Using a slotted spoon, transfer the meatballs to a saucepan.

3 In a jug, mix together the yogurt, sugar, chilli powder, the remaining garam masala and salt and the measured water. Pour the yogurt mixture over the meatballs, then cook the curry, uncovered, over a medium heat for 10 minutes, or until the meatballs are cooked and most of the liquid has been absorbed, leaving just a little sauce.

4 Garnish with ground cardamom and coriander sprigs and serve hot with nanns or parathas.

PREP
20

COOK
20

SERVES
4

creamy

Roghan ghosht

This popular Indian curry originated in Kashmir, in the north of the country. There are plenty of fresh herbs and spices and the yogurt adds a creamy finish to the dish.

1 Heat 2 tablespoons of the oil in a large saucepan, add half of the onions and fry until golden. Add the lamb and 175 ml (6 fl oz) of the yogurt, stir well, then cover and simmer for 20 minutes.

2 Meanwhile, place the spice paste ingredients in a blender or food processor and blend to a smooth paste.

3 Heat the remaining oil in a large saucepan, add the cardamom, cloves and cinnamon and fry quickly for 1 minute, stirring. Add the remaining onion and the prepared spice paste and fry for 5 minutes, stirring constantly. Add the lamb and yogurt mixture, season to taste, stir well and bring to simmering point. Cover and cook for 30 minutes.

4 Add the almonds and cook for a further 15 minutes, until the meat is tender. Remove the whole spices before serving. Garnish with fried onion rings and lemon slices and serve immediately.

PREP 20

COOK 75

SERVES 4

creamy

4 tablespoons **oil**

2 **onions**, finely chopped

750 g (1½ lb) boned **leg of lamb**, cubed

175 ml (6 fl oz) **natural yogurt**

6 **cardamom pods**, crushed

6 **cloves**

2.5 cm (1 inch) piece of **cinnamon stick**

125 g (4 oz) **flaked almonds**

salt and **pepper**

SPICE PASTE:

2 **garlic cloves**

2.5 cm (1 inch) piece of fresh **root ginger**, peeled and roughly chopped

2 **green chillies**, deseeded

1 tablespoon **coriander seeds**

1 teaspoon **cumin seeds**

1 teaspoon chopped **mint leaves**

1 teaspoon chopped **coriander**

2–3 tablespoons **natural yogurt**

TO GARNISH:

fried **onion rings**

slices of **lemon**

3 tablespoons **vegetable oil** or **ghee**

2 **onions**, finely chopped

1 teaspoon **turmeric**

1 tablespoon **ground coriander**

1 teaspoon **ground cumin**

2 teaspoons **chilli powder**

½ teaspoon **ground cloves**

12 **curry leaves**

750 g (1½ lb) boned **leg of lamb**, cubed

1 tablespoon coarsely grated **coconut**

300 ml (½ pint) **water**

1 teaspoon **salt**

Malabar lamb curry

Malabar is in the south of India. The region is now a popular holiday destination and is also known for its distinctive cuisine.

1 Heat the oil or ghee in a saucepan. Add the onions and fry until golden. Stir in the turmeric, coriander, cumin, chilli powder, cloves and curry leaves and fry for 1–2 minutes.

2 Add the lamb and coconut and fry, stirring, until the meat is well browned. Pour in the measured water and add the salt. Cover and simmer for 45 minutes or until the lamb is tender.

3 Transfer the lamb curry to a warmed serving dish and serve immediately.

PREP **5**

COOK **55**

SERVES **4**

spicy

Balti lamb madras

This hot lamb curry would make a great midweek meal as it is really quick to prepare and contains lots of store cupboard ingredients.

1 Heat the oil in a preheated wok or heavy-based frying pan. Add the chopped onion, garlic, chillies and chilli powder and stir-fry for 2 minutes. Add the garam masala, cubed lamb, vinegar, salt and chopped tomatoes. Stir the mixture thoroughly.

2 Cover the wok and cook over a moderate heat for 30–40 minutes until the lamb is tender, adding a little water if it appears to be sticking to the base of the wok.

3 Transfer to a warmed serving dish, scatter with the coconut flakes and serve immediately.

1 tablespoon **vegetable oil**

1 **onion**, chopped

2 **garlic cloves**, crushed

2 **green chillies**, deseeded and sliced

2 teaspoons **chilli powder**

2 teaspoons **garam masala**

500 g (1 lb) lean **lamb**, cut into 3.5 cm (1½ inch) cubes

1 tablespoon **vinegar**

1 teaspoon **salt**

2 **tomatoes**, skinned, deseeded and chopped

TO GARNISH:

1 tablespoon **coconut flakes**

PREP
10

COOK
45

SERVES
4

hot

50 g (2 oz) **lentils**

50 g (2 oz) **split yellow lentils** (moong dhal)

50 g (2 oz) **chickpeas**

750 g (1½ lb) **lamb fillet**, cut into 5 cm (2 inch) cubes

300 g (10 oz) **aubergine**, cubed

250 g (8 oz) **pumpkin**, peeled, deseeded and cubed

125 g (4 oz) **potato**, peeled and cubed

2 **onions**, roughly chopped, and 1 large, thinly sliced

2 **tomatoes**, skinned and chopped

75 g (3 oz) **spinach**, washed

3 tablespoons **ghee**

2 tablespoons **tomato purée**

300 ml (½ pint) **water**

salt and **pepper**

MASALA PASTE:

3 **red chillies**, deseeded and chopped

3 **green chillies**, deseeded and chopped

6 **garlic cloves**, crushed

2.5 cm (1 inch) piece of fresh **root ginger**, peeled and finely chopped

continued opposite …

Lamb and vegetable curry

A spicy curry that is cooked with lentils in masala and a dry spice mixture.

1 Wash all the lentils and chickpeas in several changes of cold water and leave them to soak overnight in a large bowl of cold water.

2 The next day, drain the pulses and place them in a large pan with the cubed lamb. Pour over enough boiling water to cover and season generously with salt. Bring to the boil, skim any scum from the surface, then cover and simmer stirring occasionally, for about 20 minutes.

3 Add the aubergine, pumpkin, potato, the 2 roughly chopped onions, tomatoes and spinach to the pan, stir well and continue cooking for a further 40 minutes, until the pulses and vegetables are cooked and the lamb is tender. Drain the liquid from the pan and remove the pieces of meat using a slotted spoon. Set the meat aside and tip the cooked vegetables and pulses into a blender or food processor. Blend to produce a thick purée. Tip into a bowl and set aside.

PREP
40*

COOK
105

SERVES
6

hearty

* plus overnight soaking

4 Heat the ghee in a large, heavy-based frying pan and fry the thinly sliced onion over a gentle heat for 5 minutes, until softened and golden.

5 Place the masala paste ingredients in a blender or food processor and blend to a smooth paste. Add this paste to the softened onion in the frying pan and cook over a low heat for a further 3 minutes. Stir in the dry spice mixture and cook, stirring constantly, for 3 minutes, until the mixture is aromatic.

6 Return the pieces of lamb and the pulse and vegetable purée to the pan, together with the tomato purée and the measured water. Season with salt and pepper, cover and simmer the curry for about 30 minutes until it is thick. If it becomes too dry during cooking, add a little more water to the pan. Taste and adjust the seasoning if necessary.

7 Transfer the curry to a warmed serving dish. Garnish with coriander sprigs, deep-fried onion rings and chilli rings and serve immediately with the rice.

25 g (1 oz) **coriander leaves**

15 g (½ oz) **mint leaves**

4 tablespoons **water**

DRY SPICE MIXTURE:

2 teaspoons **turmeric**

1 teaspoon **black mustard seeds**

½ teaspoon **cinnamon**

¼ teaspoon **fenugreek powder**

2 tablespoons **dhana jeera powder** (see page 17)

4 **cardamom pods**, crushed

TO GARNISH:

sprigs of **coriander**

deep-fried **onion rings**

red chillies, cut into rings

TO SERVE:

Saffron and Cardamom Rice (page 212)

Lamb doh piaza

3 tablespoons **ghee**

4 tablespoons **vegetable oil**

500 g (1 lb) **onions**, sliced thinly

750 g (1½ lb) boneless **leg** or **shoulder of lamb**, cut into bite-sized pieces

150 ml (¼ pint) **natural yogurt**

SPICE MIXTURE:

1 large **onion**, finely chopped

4 **garlic cloves**, crushed

2 teaspoons peeled and freshly grated **root ginger**

1 teaspoon **turmeric**

1 teaspoon **garam masala**

2 teaspoons **chilli powder**

1 tablespoon **ground coriander**

1 tablespoon **ground cumin**

1 teaspoon **salt**

6 **cardamom pods**, bruised

TO GARNISH:

2 tablespoons chopped **coriander leaves**

Doh means two and piaza means onions, and onions are used in two ways in this recipe: finely chopped in the spice mixture and also sliced, fried and added towards the end of the cooking time.

1 Melt 2 tablespoons of the ghee in a wide, heavy-based saucepan. Add 2 tablespoons of the oil and stir in the sliced onions. Fry the onions over a medium heat, stirring frequently, for about 10 minutes or until they are browned all over. Remove the onions from the pan and set aside.

2 Add the remaining ghee and 1 more tablespoon of oil to the pan and fry the lamb in batches until browned. Remove the lamb and set aside.

3 Next add the remaining oil and all the spice mixture ingredients to the pan. Cook, stirring, for 1 minute, then stir in the yogurt and cook for a further minute.

4 Return the lamb to the pan. Stir well, cover and cook over a low heat, stirring occasionally, for 30 minutes until the meat is tender. (If the sauce appears to be drying out add a little water.)

5 Stir the reserved onions into the curry. Cover the pan and cook gently for a further 10 minutes. Taste and add more salt if necessary. Serve hot, garnished with coriander.

PREP **30** COOK **60** SERVES **4–6** creamy

Pork and bamboo shoots in sauce

This is an everyday Burmese pork dish that is served at home as part of a simple family meal with a soup, a vegetable dish, plain rice and green tea. For the best flavour choose fresh bamboo shoots from oriental stores.

1 Place the pork fillet in a non-metallic bowl. Mix the chilli powder and turmeric together and rub into the sliced pork. Set aside for 30 minutes to allow the pork to marinate.

2 Heat the oil in a large, heavy-based saucepan and gently fry the onions and garlic for 10–15 minutes or until golden brown. Add the lemon grass, galangal, red chillies and shrimp paste and fry for 2–3 minutes, stirring constantly.

3 Add the pork to the pan and fry on all sides for 3–4 minutes or until the meat has sealed. Add the tamarind liquid and stock and simmer for 8 minutes.

4 Stir in the bamboo shoots, the ground fish, if using, and season with salt and pepper. Simmer gently for 5 minutes. Serve with the balachaung and coriander leaves.

750 g (1¼ lb) **pork fillet**, thinly sliced

1 teaspoon **chilli powder**

1 teaspoon **turmeric**

3 tablespoons **vegetable oil**

2 **onions**, chopped

6 **garlic cloves**, crushed

2 **lemon grass stalks**, finely chopped

5 cm (2 inch) piece of fresh **galangal** or fresh **root ginger**, peeled and sliced

2 **red chillies**, chopped

1 teaspoon **shrimp paste**

6 tablespoons **tamarind liquid** (see page 17)

300 ml (½ pint) **chicken stock** or **water**

175 g (6 oz) can **bamboo shoots**, drained

1–2 tablespoons **ground fish** (optional)

salt and **pepper**

TO SERVE:

2–3 table spoons **balachaung** (see page 10)

handful of **coriander leaves**

PREP
20*

COOK
35

SERVES
4

tangy

* plus 30 minutes marinating

1 tablespoon **sunflower oil**

2 **garlic cloves**, finely chopped

2 **green chillies**, deseeded and finely chopped

1 teaspoon **ground coriander**

500 g (1 lb) **minced pork**

400 g (13 oz) **peas**

3 tablespoons **medium curry paste**

3 tablespoons **tomato purée**

2 **tomatoes**, finely chopped

1 teaspoon **golden caster sugar**

250 ml (8 fl oz) boiling **water**

2 tablespoons **natural yogurt**

large handful of chopped **coriander leaves**

salt

TO SERVE:

flatbreads

Pork kheema with peas

Warm, fragrant coriander, aromatic garlic and spicy chillies are the perfect partners for mildly flavoured pork. This tasty dish, in a rich tomato sauce, is quick and easy to make and is great for a simple mid-week supper.

1 Heat the oil in a large, nonstick wok or frying pan and when it is hot add the garlic, chillies, ground coriander and pork. Stir-fry over a high heat for 4–5 minutes until the meat is sealed and lightly browned.

2 Stir in the peas, curry paste, tomato purée, chopped tomatoes and sugar. Stir and cook for 3–4 minutes, then add the measured water. Bring to the boil, cover, reduce the heat and cook gently for 8–10 minutes or until the meat is tender. Remove from the heat, stir in the yogurt and the chopped coriander and season. Serve with flatbreads.

PREP **10** COOK **20** SERVES **4** hot

Dry pork curry

This is a delicious way to prepare pork. As this dish is not cooked in a sauce, it can be served with any number of accompaniments.

1 Slit the pork fillets lengthways and cut each half into quarters. Prick the pieces all over with a fork. Roughly pound the coriander with a pestle and mortar, then mix it together with the pepper, paprika and salt to taste and rub into the meat on both sides. Leave to marinate for 1 hour.

2 Heat the oil in a pan, add the meat and fry quickly on both sides to seal. Reduce the heat and sauté for 5 minutes or until cooked through, stirring and turning to prevent it burning.

3 Sprinkle with the coriander, if liked, and serve with a tomato and red onion salad.

750 g (1¼ lb) **pork fillets**

2 tablespoons **coriander seeds**

1 teaspoon **pepper**

1 tablespoon **paprika**

4 tablespoons **vegetable oil**

salt

TO GARNISH:

2 tablespoons finely chopped **coriander leaves** (optional)

TO SERVE:

tomato and **red onion salad**

PREP **15***

COOK **10**

SERVES **4**

dry

* plus 1 hour marinating

750 g (1½ lb) **pork fillet** or **tenderloin**, cubed

200 ml (7 fl oz) **vinegar**

2–6 teaspoons **chilli powder**

2 teaspoons **coriander seeds**

1 teaspoon **white cumin seeds**

10 cm (4 inch) piece of **cinnamon stick**

12 **cloves**

12 **green cardamom pods**

2 teaspoons **pepper**

4 tablespoons **ghee**

1 quantity **curry purée** (see page 24)

4–8 fresh or dried **red chillies**

salt

TO GARNISH:

sprigs of **basil**

Goan vindaloo

A hot pork curry cooked with dry-fried spices, chilli powder and chillies.

1 Place the pork in a non-metallic dish with the vinegar and a quantity of chilli powder according to your taste. Cover and refrigerate for 24 hours.

2 Dry-fry the spices in a frying pan, shaking the pan over a fairly high heat for 1–2 minutes. Cool slightly, then grind them using a pestle and mortar or an electric spice mill and mix with enough water to make a paste.

3 Heat the ghee in a large frying pan or wok and stir-fry the curry purée for 5 minutes. Add the spice paste, stir-frying for 2 minutes more. Lift the pieces of pork out of the marinade, reserving the liquid, and combine them with the ingredients in the frying pan.

4 Transfer the mixture to a heavy-lidded casserole and bake in a preheated oven, 190°C (375°F), Gas Mark 5, for 1 hour, adding the red chillies to taste after 20 minutes of cooking time, with a little salt and some marinade to moisten if necessary. If, at the end of the cooking time, there is an excess of oil, spoon it off before serving. Garnish with sprigs of basil.

PREP **15***

COOK **90**

SERVES **4**

fiery

* plus 24 hours marinating

Burmese pork curry

Ginger, palm sugar and shrimp paste combine to produce a wonderfully fragrant and flavoursome sauce in this Burmese dish.

1 Heat the ghee in a heavy-based saucepan, add the onion, garlic, ginger and pork, and fry over a brisk heat, stirring constantly, for 4 minutes until lightly golden.

2 Lower the heat, stir in the turmeric, sugar, curry paste, shrimp paste, dried chillies and lemon grass, and fry for a further 2 minutes.

3 Add the stock and soy sauce to the pan, stir to mix well, then bring the curry to the boil. Cover the pan, reduce the heat and cook the curry gently for 30 minutes, stirring occasionally, until the pork is tender. Discard the lemon grass and taste and adjust the seasoning, if necessary. Serve the curry hot, garnished with sliced red chillies.

2 tablespoons **ghee**

2 small **onions**, each cut into 8 wedges

4 **garlic cloves**, finely chopped

5 cm (2 inch) piece of fresh **root ginger**, peeled and finely chopped

500 g (1 lb) **pork tenderloin**, cut into 2.5 cm (1 inch) cubes

1 teaspoon **turmeric**

½ teaspoon **palm sugar** or **soft brown sugar**

1 tablespoon **mild curry paste** (see page 17)

1 teaspoon **shrimp paste**

4 **dried chillies**, soaked in cold water for 10 minutes, then drained and finely chopped

2 **lemon grass stalks**, quartered lengthways

150 ml (¼ pint) **vegetable stock**

2 teaspoons **soy sauce**

TO GARNISH:

2 **red chillies**, deseeded and thinly sliced

PREP 10

COOK 45

SERVES 4

fresh

Thai pork curry

2 tablespoons **groundnut oil**

2 **shallots**, sliced

1 **green chilli**, deseeded and sliced

500 g (1 lb) **pork tenderloin**, cut into bite-sized pieces

1 tablespoon **fish sauce**

¼ teaspoon **palm sugar** or **soft brown sugar**

150 ml (¼ pint) **coconut milk**

75 g (3 oz) canned **bamboo shoots**, drained

2 tablespoons chopped **coriander leaves**

CURRY PASTE:

2 large **dried red chillies**, deseeded and chopped

3 **garlic cloves**, crushed

2 **kaffir lime leaves**, chopped

6 **black peppercorns**, crushed

1 tablespoon chopped **lemon grass stalk**

½ teaspoon **shrimp paste**

TO GARNISH:

1 **green chilli**, cut into rings

TO SERVE:

steamed **jasmine rice**

Groundnut oil has a distinctive flavour that is essential to this dish. It is worth sourcing palm sugar if you intend to cook a lot of Thai food.

1 Place the curry paste ingredients in a blender or food processor and blend to a thick paste.

2 Heat the oil in a heavy-based saucepan, add the shallots and chilli and fry over a gentle heat, stirring, for 3 minutes. Stir in the curry paste and fry for a further 1 minute.

3 Add the pork to the pan, stir to coat it evenly in the spice mixture, then stir in the fish sauce and sugar. Cook, stirring, for 3 minutes. Add the coconut milk to the pan, bring the curry to the boil, then lower the heat and simmer gently for 20 minutes, stirring just occasionally, until the pork is tender.

4 Stir in the bamboo shoots and coriander. Cook for 2 minutes to heat through. Garnish with chilli rings and serve hot with steamed jasmine rice.

PREP 25

COOK 30

SERVES 4

creamy

Sri Lankan fried pork curry

This type of curry is called Badun in Sri Lanka – it is rich, dark and full of flavour.

1 Heat 2 tablespoons of the oil in a heavy-based pan, add the fenugreek and curry leaves. Fry gently for 2 minutes.

2 Place the onion, garlic and ginger in a blender or food processor and blend to a paste. Add to the pan and fry, stirring occasionally, for 5 minutes.

3 Add the spice mixture, chilli powder, salt, vinegar and pork. Mix well and then increase the heat and cook, stirring frequently for 8 minutes. Stir in the cinnamon, cardamom, sugar and the measured water, cover and simmer gently for 30 minutes, stirring occasionally.

4 Stir in the coconut milk and increase the heat. Cook uncovered for a further 10 minutes, stirring frequently.

5 Using a slotted spoon, remove the pieces of pork from the sauce. Heat the remaining oil in a heavy-based frying pan and add the pork. Fry the pork, turning it frequently for 8 minutes or until it is browned all over.

6 Drain off the oil and return the pork to the sauce. Simmer for 10 minutes or until you have a dark sauce.

4 tablespoons **vegetable oil**

¼ teaspoon **fenugreek seeds**

5 **curry leaves**

1 large **onion**, chopped

3 **garlic cloves**, crushed

2.5 cm (1 inch) piece of fresh **root ginger**, peeled and chopped

2 tablespoons **Sri Lankan spice mixture** (see page 113)

1 teaspoon **chilli powder**

1 teaspoon **salt**

3 tablespoons **malt vinegar**

625 g (1¼ lb) **pork tenderloin**, cut into 5 cm (2 inch) pieces

2.5 cm (1 inch) piece of **cinnamon stick**

4 **cardamom pods**, bruised

1 teaspoon **palm sugar** or **soft brown sugar**

150 ml (¼ pint) **water**

300 ml (½ pint) **coconut milk**

PREP **30** COOK **60** SERVES **4–6** rich

chicken and duck

6 tablespoons ready-made **tikka curry paste**

75 ml (3 fl oz) **natural yogurt**

1 tablespoon **vegetable oil**

750 g (1½ lb) boneless, skinless **chicken breasts**, cut into cubes

MASALA SAUCE:

4 tablespoons **ghee**

2 tablespoons ready-made **medium curry paste**

1 tablespoon **tandoori paste**

2 teaspoons **tomato purée**

2 **tomatoes**, skinned and chopped

1 **red pepper**, cored, deseeded and chopped

1 tablespoon **coriander leaves**, chopped

1 tablespoon **ground almonds**

2 tablespoons **single cream**

pinch of **sugar**

salt

TO SERVE:

rice and **nann bread**

Chicken tikka masala

You can also make this delicious Indian speciality with fish rather than chicken – just make sure you choose firm white fish such as cod or haddock.

1 Mix the curry paste with the yogurt and oil, then coat the chicken with it. Place in a non-metallic bowl, cover and put in the refridgerator for at least 6 hours, or overnight. Put 2 tablespoons of the marinade in a bowl to use later.

2 Take the pieces of chicken out of the marinade and spear onto skewers. Grill for 10–15 minutes under a preheated grill, turning 2 or 3 times.

3 Meanwhile, make the masala sauce. Heat the ghee in a frying pan. Fry the curry paste for 5 minutes. Add the tandoori paste and the 2 tablespoons extra marinade and fry for 2 minutes. Add the tomato purée, tomatoes and red pepper and simmer. Add a little water to make a creamy sauce, plus the coriander, almonds, cream and sugar and a dash of salt.

4 When the tikkas are cooked, take them off the skewers and stir into the sauce. Eat with rice and nann bread.

PREP **30***

COOK **25**

SERVES **4**

mild

* plus at least 6 hours marinating

Chicken korma with green beans

A classic creamy chicken dish that is perfect for those who don't like too much heat in their curries.

1 Heat the oil in a saucepan, add the chicken and onion, and fry over a gentle heat, stirring occasionally, for 6 minutes or until the onion is soft and the chicken is lightly coloured. Stir in the curry powder and cook for a further 2 minutes.

2 Add the stock, tomato purée, sugar, tomatoes, cream and a little salt. Stir to combine the ingredients, bring to the boil, then reduce the heat, cover the pan and simmer gently for 10 minutes, stirring occasionally.

3 Stir the beans into the curry and cook, covered, for a further 15–20 minutes, stirring occasionally, until the chicken is cooked through and the beans are tender. Stir the ground almonds into the curry and simmer for 1 minute to thicken the sauce. Taste and adjust the seasoning if necessary. Serve the korma hot, garnished with toasted flaked almonds.

2 tablespoons **vegetable oil**

375 g (12 oz) boneless, skinless **chicken breasts**, cut into bite-sized pieces

1 **onion**, sliced

2½ tablespoons **korma curry powder**

150 ml (¼ pint) **chicken stock**

1 teaspoon **tomato purée**

2 teaspoons **caster sugar**

75 g (3 oz) **tomatoes**, roughly chopped

150 ml (¼ pint) **single cream**

125 g (4 oz) **green beans**, trimmed and cut into 2.5 cm (1 inch) lengths

25 g (1 oz) **ground almonds**

salt

TO GARNISH:

toasted flaked **almonds**

PREP
15

COOK
40

SERVES
4

creamy

Chicken bhuna

3 tablespoons **ghee**

8 **dried curry leaves**

1 teaspoon **black mustard seeds**

1 large **onion**, chopped

4 **garlic cloves**, chopped

2.5 cm (1 inch) piece of fresh **root ginger**, peeled and chopped

1 tablespoon **curry powder**

1 teaspoon **garam masala**

1 teaspoon **ground cumin**

1 teaspoon **ground coriander**

2 teaspoons **chilli powder**

750 g (1½ lb) skinless, boneless **chicken breasts** or **thighs**, cut into 2.5 cm (1 inch) cubes

1 teaspoon **salt**

150 ml (¼ pint) **water**

Serve this dry chicken curry with Indian flatbreads, such as chapati or paratha.

1 Heat the ghee in a heavy-based frying pan, crumble the curry leaves and add them to the pan with the mustard seeds. Fry them over a gentle heat for 1 minute.

2 Place the onion, garlic and ginger in a blender or food processor and blend to a coarse paste. Add this paste to the fried curry leaves and mustard seeds and cook gently for a further 5 minutes.

3 Add the curry powder, garam masala, cumin, ground coriander and chilli powder to the pan, and cook, stirring, for 2 minutes.

4 Add the chicken, salt and measured water. Stir to coat the chicken evenly in the spice mixture, then cover the pan and cook over a gentle heat, stirring occasionally, for 20 minutes, or until the chicken is tender.

5 Remove the lid, increase the heat and cook the curry for a further 3–5 minutes, until thick and dry. Taste and adjust the seasoning if necessary and serve the curry immediately.

PREP **10**   COOK **35**   SERVES **4–6**   spicy

Chicken jalfrezi

This is a mild variation of the classic jalfrezi dish. It is quite a dry dish but the flavours are incredible.

1 Heat the butter or ghee in a large frying pan or wok and stir-fry the cumin and mustard seeds for 1 minute. Add the garlic and stir-fry for 1 minute more. Add the ginger and stir-fry for 2 minutes. Add the sliced onion and stir-fry for about 5 minutes until golden.

2 Combine the chicken with the spice mixture in the pan and stir-fry for 5 minutes.

3 Add the curry paste, red and green peppers, tomatoes, coriander and measured water and stir-fry for around 10 minutes more. Garnish with coriander sprigs and serve.

6 tablespoons clarified butter or **ghee**

1 teaspoon **white cumin seeds**

1 teaspoon **black mustard seeds**

2–6 **garlic cloves**, finely chopped

5 cm (2 inch) piece of fresh **root ginger**, peeled and finely sliced

1 large **onion**, thinly sliced

750 g (1½ lb) boneless, skinless **chicken breasts**, diced

1 tablespoon **mild curry paste** (see page 17)

½ **red pepper**, cored, deseeded and chopped

½ **green pepper**, cored, deseeded and chopped

2 **tomatoes**, skinned and chopped

1 tablespoon chopped **coriander leaves**

1–2 tablespoons **water**

TO GARNISH:

sprigs of **coriander**

PREP **10**

COOK **25**

SERVES **4**

dry

250 g (8 oz) **split yellow lentils** (moong dhal)

600 ml (1 pint) **water**

4 tablespoons chopped **coriander leaves**

2 large **onions**, chopped

125 g (4 oz) **pumpkin**, peeled, deseeded and diced

150 g (5 oz) **aubergine**, diced

125 g (4 oz) **potatoes**, diced

4 tablespoons **vegetable oil**

1 teaspoon **garam masala**

750 g (1½ lb) skinless, boneless **chicken breasts**, cubed

5 cm (2 inch) piece of fresh **root ginger**, peeled and grated

6 **garlic cloves**, crushed

4 tablespoons chopped **fenugreek leaves**

4 large **tomatoes**, chopped

4 large **green chillies**, finely chopped

2 teaspoons **tomato purée**

1 tablespoon **palm sugar** or **soft brown sugar**

150 ml (¼ pint) **tamarind liquid** (see page 17)

300 ml (½ pint) **chicken stock**

continued opposite …

Chicken dhansak

Dhansak is a meat, vegetable and lentil curry made with puréed lentils, aubergines, tomatoes and fenugreek leaves, but spinach can be substituted. A Parsee dish, it is eaten with pulao rice and often served at family meals.

1 Wash the lentils in several changes of cold water and leave them to soak overnight in a large bowl of cold water.

2 Heat a dry frying pan until hot and add the spice mixture ingredients. Dry-fry for 4–5 minutes or until the spices are toasted and releasing their aroma.

3 Place the drained lentils in a saucepan with the measured water, 1 tablespoon of the chopped coriander, 2 teaspoons of the toasted spice mixture, the onions, pumpkin, aubergine and potatoes. Simmer, covered, for 40 minutes or until the vegetables and lentils are very soft. Remove from the heat and purée to a smooth sauce.

4 Meanwhile, heat the oil and fry the remaining spice mixture with the garam masala. Add the chicken and fry on all sides to seal.

PREP
25*

COOK
90

SERVES
4

hearty

* plus overnight soaking

5 Add the ginger, garlic, the remaining chopped coriander, fenugreek leaves, tomatoes and green chillies to the pan and cook for 10 minutes.

6 Add the puréed lentil mixture to the chicken with the tomato purée, sugar, tamarind liquid and stock. Simmer gently, covered, for 35 minutes or until the chicken has cooked through and is tender. Season to taste with salt and pepper and add the vinegar and lemon juice. Simmer for 5 minutes and serve.

1 teaspoon **white wine vinegar**

juice of 1 **lemon**

salt and **pepper**

SPICE MIXTURE:

seeds from 3 **cardamom pods**

¼ teaspoon **cloves**

¼ teaspoon **ground nutmeg**

½ teaspoon **ground star anise**

1 tablespoon **ground coriander**

½ teaspoon **ground fenugreek**

1 teaspoon **chilli powder**

½ teaspoon **pepper**

2 tablespoons **vindaloo masala**

2 teaspoons **vinegar**

3 teaspoons **salt**

1.5 kg (3 lb) **chicken**, cut into pieces

6 tablespoons **mustard oil** or **vegetable oil**

4 **bay leaves**

1 teaspoon **green cardamom seeds**

1 large **onion**, thinly sliced

2 teaspoons **turmeric**

1 teaspoon **cayenne**

10 **garlic cloves**, crushed

15 g (½ oz) fresh **root ginger**, peeled and thinly sliced

2 **tomatoes**, skinned and quartered

150 ml (¼ pint) **tamarind liquid** (see page 17) or **lemon juice**

TO GARNISH:

2 teaspoons **desiccated coconut**

Chicken vindaloo

A chicken vindaloo is a fiery curry, and strictly not for the fainthearted! If you're worried about it being too hot, reduce the quantity of vindaloo masala.

1 Put the vindaloo masala, vinegar and 2 teaspoons of the salt in a bowl and mix well to make a smooth paste.

2 Wash and dry the chicken pieces and score each piece several times with a sharp knife. Rub the paste all over them and leave in a cool place to marinate for 1 hour.

3 Heat the mustard oil in a large saucepan and stir in the bay leaves and cardamom seeds. Add the onion and fry until light brown. Stir in the turmeric and cayenne and add the chicken pieces. Cook, stirring occasionally, for 15 minutes. Add the reserved salt, garlic, ginger and tomatoes and cook for 10 minutes, stirring.

4 Add the tamarind or lemon juice to the pan when the fat starts to separate. Stir well, cover and simmer gently for about 25 minutes or until the chicken is tender. Garnish with coconut and serve.

PREP
15*

COOK
55

SERVES
6

fiery

* plus 1 hour marinating

Chicken and spinach masala

Chicken and spinach are a classic curry combination and this fragrant Indian recipe uses a variety of spices and crème fraîche to enrich the sauce.

1 Heat the oil in a large heavy-based saucepan. Add the onion, garlic, chilli and ginger. Stir-fry for 2–3 minutes and then add the ground coriander and cumin. Stir and cook for 1 minute.

2 Pour in the tomatoes with their juice and cook gently for 3 minutes. Increase the heat and add the chicken. Cook, stirring, until the chicken pieces are sealed. Stir in the crème fraîche and spinach.

3 Cover the pan and cook the chicken mixture gently for 6–8 minutes, stirring occasionally. Stir in the coriander with salt and pepper to taste. Serve hot with nann bread or basmati rice, chutneys or a mixed salad.

2 tablespoons **vegetable oil**

1 **onion**, thinly sliced

2 **garlic cloves**, crushed

1 **green chilli**, deseeded and thinly sliced

1 teaspoon peeled and finely grated fresh **root ginger**

1 teaspoon **ground coriander**

1 teaspoon **ground cumin**

200 g (7 oz) can **tomatoes**

750 g (1¾ lb) **chicken thighs**, skinned, boned and cut into bite-sized pieces

200 ml (7 fl oz) **crème fraîche**

300 g (10 oz) **spinach**, roughly chopped

2 tablespoons chopped **coriander leaves**

salt and **pepper**

TO SERVE:

warmed **nann bread** or boiled **basmati rice**

chutneys or **fresh mixed salad**

PREP
15

COOK
20

SERVES
4

rich

Opor ayam

2 kg (4 lb) **chicken**, cut into 8 pieces

4 tablespoons **vegetable oil**

2 **onions**, thinly sliced

450 ml (¾ pint) **coconut milk**

300 ml (½ pint) **water**

1 **lemon grass stalk**, bruised

5 cm (2 inch) piece of **cinnamon stick**

4 **dried curry leaves**

1 teaspoon **lemon juice**

SPICE PASTE:

4 **garlic cloves**, crushed

2.5 cm (1 inch) piece of fresh **root ginger**, peeled and chopped

2 tablespoons finely chopped **Brazil nuts**

1 tablespoon **ground coriander**

2 teaspoons **ground cumin**

2 teaspoons chopped fresh **galangal**

1 teaspoon **salt**

½ teaspoon **fennel seeds**, crushed

¼ teaspoon **pepper**

1 tablespoon **vegetable oil**

TO GARNISH:

fried **onion rings**

The English translation for this dish is chicken and coconut milk curry.

1 Place the spice paste ingredients in a blender or spice mill and blend to a thick paste. Rub the paste over the chicken pieces and place in a non-metallic dish. Cover and marinate for 2 hours.

2 Heat 2 tablespoons of the oil in a sauté pan. Add the onions and fry over a moderate heat, stirring frequently, for 10 minutes or until softened and golden. Remove with a slotted spoon; drain on kitchen paper.

3 Add the remaining oil to the pan and stir in the chicken. Fry over a low heat for 15 minutes, turning occasionally, until pale golden. Remove the chicken from the pan, stir in 300 ml (½ pint) of the coconut milk and the measured water. Add the lemon grass, cinnamon and curry leaves, bring to the boil, then return the chicken to the pan and cook, uncovered, over a low heat for 40 minutes.

4 Stir in the remaining coconut milk and lemon juice, and cook for 10 minutes. Serve hot, garnished with the onions.

PREP
20*

COOK
80

SERVES
4

creamy

* plus 2 hours marinating

Chicken and sweet potato curry

This is a delicious Vietnamese curry with a sweet flavour due to the addition of the sweet potato.

1 Place the spice paste ingredients in a blender or food processor and blend to a thick paste. Set aside.

2 Cook the potato in a pan of boiling, salted water for 8–10 minutes until tender. Drain and set aside.

3 Heat the oil in a wok. Add the spice paste and fry over a gentle heat, stirring for about 5 minutes, until softened but not coloured. Stir in the curry powder, turmeric and chilli flakes and fry for a further 2 minutes.

4 Add the chicken to the wok, stir to coat it evenly in the spice mixture and fry, stirring, for 2 minutes. Add the stock, bring it to the boil, then reduce the heat and simmer gently for 10 minutes or until most of the stock has evaporated.

5 Stir in the coconut milk, salt and pepper and cook the curry gently, stirring occasionally, for a further 10 minutes. Stir the cooked sweet potato into the curry and heat through for 3–4 minutes. Taste and adjust the seasoning if necessary. Garnish the curry with spring onion slices and serve.

PREP **15**

COOK **45**

SERVES **4–6**

sweet

500 g (1 lb) **sweet potato**, peeled and cut into 2.5 cm (1 inch) chunks

4 tablespoons **groundnut oil**

1 tablespoon **hot curry powder**

1 teaspoon **turmeric**

1 teaspoon dried **chilli flakes**

500 g (1 lb) boneless, skinless **chicken breasts**, cut into bite-sized pieces

300 ml (½ pint) **chicken stock**

150 ml (¼ pint) **coconut milk**

½ teaspoon **salt**

pepper

SPICE PASTE:

1 large **onion**, roughly chopped

3 **garlic cloves**, chopped

1 **lemon grass stalk**, finely chopped

TO GARNISH:

3 **spring onions**, cut into julienne slices

Thai green curry with chicken

2 tablespoons **vegetable oil**

2.5 cm (1 inch) piece of fresh **root ginger**, peeled and finely chopped

1 small **onion** or 2 **shallots**, chopped

4 tablespoons **green curry paste** (see page 15)

625 g (1¼ lb) boneless, skinless **chicken thighs**, cut into chunks

300 ml (½ pint) **coconut milk**

4 teaspoons **fish sauce**

1 teaspoon **sugar**

3 **kaffir lime leaves**, shredded

1 **green chilli**, deseeded and sliced

salt and **pepper**

Green curries are spicy yet soothing due to the great mix of chilli and creamy coconut milk. This is a quick version that tastes delicious.

1   Heat the oil in a wok or large frying pan, toss in the ginger and shallots and fry over a gentle heat, stirring, for about 3 minutes or until soft. Add the curry paste and fry for another 2 minutes.

2   Add the chicken to the wok or frying pan, stir well and fry for 3 minutes. Stir in the coconut milk, bring to the boil, then turn down the heat and cook the curry gently, stirring occasionally, for 10 minutes or until the chicken is cooked and the sauce is thick.

3   Stir in the fish sauce, sugar, lime leaves and chilli and cook the curry for another 5 minutes. Taste and add salt and pepper if it needs it, then serve.

PREP
10

COOK
25

SERVES
4

spicy

Chicken and dhal curry

Chicken thighs work really well in curries, because they need lengthy cooking, and preferably in a sauce, to tenderise the meat.

1 Wash the lentils in several changes of cold water, then leave to soak in a bowl of clean water for 1 hour. Drain the lentils and boil in the measured water with 1 teaspoon salt added, for about 1 hour, until soft. Drain and set aside.

2 Heat the oil in a pan, add the onions, garlic and ginger and fry for about 5 minutes. Add the spices and salt to taste and fry gently for 10 minutes. If the mixture becomes too dry, add 2 tablespoons water. Add the chicken thighs and fry until golden all over. Add the cooked lentils, cover and simmer for about 30 minutes, or until the meat is tender.

250 g (8 oz) **red lentils** (masoor dhal)

600 ml (1 pint) **water**

3 tablespoons **vegetable oil**

2 **onions**, finely chopped

2 **garlic cloves**, crushed

2.5 cm (1 inch) piece of fresh **root ginger**, peeled and finely chopped

1 tablespoon **ground coriander**

1 teaspoon **ground cumin**

½ teaspoon **turmeric**

½ teaspoon **ground cloves**

2 teaspoons **chilli powder**

750 g (1½ lb) **chicken thighs**

salt

PREP
15*

* plus 1 hour soaking

COOK
120

SERVES
4

hearty

2 **garlic cloves**, chopped

5 cm (2 inch) piece of fresh **root ginger**, peeled and chopped

1 teaspoon **turmeric**

2 teaspoons **cumin seeds**, ground

1 teaspoon **chilli powder**

1 teaspoon **pepper**

3 tablespoons finely chopped **coriander leaves**

500 ml (17 fl oz) **natural yogurt**

1 kg (2 lb) **chicken pieces**, skinned

4 tablespoons **vegetable oil**

2 **onions**, chopped

salt

Chicken curry

A simple chicken curry that incorporates plenty of spices combined with yogurt for a rich, creamy flavour.

1 Place the garlic, ginger, turmeric, cumin, chilli powder, pepper, coriander, yogurt and salt to taste in a large bowl. Mix well, add the chicken pieces and leave for 4 hours, turning occasionally.

2 Heat the oil in a pan, add the onions and fry until golden. Add the chicken and the marinade. Bring to simmering point, cover and cook for about 30 minutes, until the chicken is tender.

PREP
10*

COOK
40

SERVES
4

creamy

* plus 4 hours marinating

Chicken korma

This mild curry, in which yogurt makes a delicately creamy sauce, is a favourite with many people who do not care for anything too hot or spicy.

1 Put the yogurt, turmeric and one of the garlic cloves in a blender or food processor and blend to a smooth purée.

2 Place the chicken pieces in a shallow, non-metallic dish and pour the yogurt mixture over them. Cover the dish and leave to marinate in the refrigerator overnight.

3 Heat the ghee or oil in a large, heavy-bottomed saucepan and add the onion and remaining garlic. Fry gently for 4–5 minutes until soft. Add the spices and salt and fry for a further 3 minutes, stirring constantly.

4 Add the chicken pieces with the yogurt marinade and coconut and mix well. Cover the pan with a tightly fitting lid and then simmer gently for 45 minutes, or until the chicken is cooked and tender. Transfer to a warmed serving dish and scatter the curry with the almonds and coriander leaves.

175 ml (6 fl oz) **natural yogurt**

2 teaspoons **turmeric**

3 **garlic cloves**, sliced

1.5 kg (3 lb) **roasting chicken**, skinned and cut into 8 pieces

125 g (4 oz) **ghee** or 4 tablespoons **vegetable oil**

1 large **onion**, sliced

1 teaspoon **ground ginger**

5 cm (2 inch) piece of **cinnamon stick**

5 **cloves**

5 **cardamom pods**

1 tablespoon crushed **coriander seeds**

1 teaspoon **ground cumin**

½ teaspoon **chilli powder**

1 teaspoon **salt**

1½ tablespoons **desiccated coconut**

TO GARNISH:

2 teaspoons **toasted almonds**

coriander leaves

PREP **15***

COOK **55**

SERVES **4**

mild

* plus overnight marinating

3 large **red chillies**, deseeded and chopped

4 **garlic cloves**, crushed

2 teaspoons toasted **cumin seeds**, crushed

1 teaspoon **garam masala**

2 tablespoons **coriander leaves**

juice of 1 **lemon**

150 ml (¼ pint) **natural yogurt**

750 g (1½ lb boneless, skinless **chicken breasts** or **thighs**, cut into 5 cm (2 inch) pieces

1.5 kg (3 lb) **tomatoes**, quartered

50 g (2 oz) **butter**

150 ml (¼ pint) **double cream**

3 tablespoons **vegetable oil**

salt

TO GARNISH:

1 tablespoon **double cream**

a few sprigs of **coriander**

TO SERVE:

nann bread

Chicken makhani

Tomatoes and butter are the characteristic ingredients of a makhani, which is a refined and elegant dish.

1 Place the chillies, garlic and cumin seeds in a blender or food processor and blend briefly before adding the garam masala, ½ teaspoon salt, coriander, lemon juice and yogurt and blending to produce a paste.

2 Transfer the marinade to a non-metallic bowl. Add the chicken pieces to the marinade, turning to coat them evenly. Cover and refrigerate for 3 hours.

3 Meanwhile, place the tomatoes in a large saucepan and cook them gently, with no added water, for about 20 minutes or until they are tender. Then rub them through a fine sieve into a clean saucepan. Simmer the tomato pulp, stirring occasionally, for about 50 minutes until it is thick and reduced.

4 Stir in the butter and some salt and cook the sauce over a medium heat, stirring often, for a further 30 minutes until it is thick. Stir in the double cream and heat it through. Taste and adjust the amount of salt if necessary and set the sauce aside.

PREP
15*

COOK
135

SERVES
6

creamy

* plus 3 hours marinating

5 Heat the oil in a large, heavy-based frying pan. Remove the chicken pieces from their marinade, reserving the marinade, and fry them gently to seal them, for about 5 minutes. Add the marinade to the pan, increase the heat and cook, stirring frequently, for a further 12 minutes or until the chicken is cooked through.

6 Reduce the heat and pour the tomato sauce over the chicken. Simmer gently for a further 5 minutes.

7 Transfer the chicken to a serving dish, garnish with a swirl of cream and a few coriander sprigs and serve with nann bread.

1.5 kg (3 lb) **chicken**, skinned and cut into pieces

3 tablespoons **vegetable oil**

12 **curry leaves**, plus extra, shredded, to garnish

1 teaspoon **cumin seeds**

SPICE PASTE:

1½ teaspoons **coriander seeds**

1½ teaspoons **cumin seeds**

¼ teaspoon **black onion seeds**

¼ teaspoon **fenugreek seeds**

¼ teaspoon **mustard seeds**

2.5 cm (1 inch) piece of **cinnamon stick**

3 **cloves**

¾ teaspoon **peppercorns**

2 tablespoons **desiccated coconut**

2 tablespoons **unsalted peanuts**

6 tablespoons **vinegar**

2 **garlic cloves**, crushed

1 teaspoon peeled and chopped fresh **root ginger**

½ teaspoon **turmeric**

1½ teaspoons **chilli powder**

2 teaspoons **salt**

TO GARNISH:

fried **onion rings**

Balti chicken vindaloo

This one isn't for the fainthearted. The best drink to serve with a really hot curry is a lassi (Indian yogurt drink) as this will help to cool down the taste buds.

1 Dry-fry all the spice paste ingredients up to and including the peanuts, then grind them in a spice grinder. Transfer to a bowl and mix in the remaining ingredients. Spread the mixture over the chicken pieces, cover and leave to marinate overnight.

2 Heat the oil in a balti pan or wok, then add the curry leaves and cumin seeds. Cook for 10 seconds, then add the chicken and cook for 15 minutes, turning once or twice. Cover and cook for a further 15–20 minutes or until the chicken is tender, adding a little water from time to time to keep the chicken moist. Leave over a very low heat for a few minutes before serving, garnished with the onion rings and some shredded curry leaves.

PREP **20***

COOK **40**

SERVES **4–6**

fiery

* plus overnight marinating

Balti chicken

This really is one-pot cooking, with the pan retaining all the wonderful aromas of the the fried spices.

1 Dry-fry the peppercorns and fennel seeds in a wok or large frying pan over a gentle heat, stirring constantly, for 2–3 minutes until fragrant. Remove, then pound to a fine powder using a pestle and mortar. Heat the oil in the same pan, add the onion, ginger and garlic and fry gently, stirring frequently, for about 5 minutes until soft.

2 Add the powdered spices, garam masala, coriander, cumin, chilli and turmeric. Stir-fry this for 2–3 minutes, then add the measured water, coconut milk powder, lemon juice and ⅛ teaspoon salt. Bring to the boil, stirring, then add the cardamoms, cinnamon and bay leaf. Simmer, stirring occasionally, for about 15–20 minutes, until a glaze forms on the liquid.

3 Add the chicken, tomatoes and sugar and stir well. Cover and cook over a gentle heat for about 40 minutes, stirring occasionally, or until the chicken feels tender when pierced with a fork.

4 Discard the bay leaf and cinnamon stick, then taste and add more salt if necessary. Serve immediately.

PREP **30**   COOK **60**   SERVES **4–6**   tasty

½ teaspoon **black peppercorns**

¼ teaspoon **fennel seeds**

2 tablespoons **vegetable oil**

1 **onion**, thinly sliced

2.5 cm (1 inch) piece of fresh **root ginger**, peeled and crushed

1 **garlic clove**, crushed

1 tablespoon **garam masala**

1 teaspoon **ground coriander**

1 teaspoon **ground cumin**

1 teaspoon **chilli powder**, or to taste

1 teaspoon **turmeric**

475 ml (16 fl oz) **water**

50 g (2 oz) **coconut milk powder**

1 tablespoon **lemon juice**

6 **cardamon pods**, bruised

5 cm (2 inch) piece of **cinnamon stick**

1 **bay leaf**

1 kg (2 lb) boneless, skinless **chicken thighs**, cut into bite-sized pieces

4 ripe **tomatoes**, skinned, deseeded and roughly chopped

¼ teaspoon **sugar**

salt

5 tablespoons **groundnut oil**

2 kg (4 lb) **chicken**, cut into 6–8 serving pieces

2 **onions**, finely chopped

1 **garlic clove**, crushed

1 **red chilli**, deseeded and finely chopped

2 tablespoons **curry powder**

250 g (8 oz) **aubergine**, peeled and cubed

1 **chayote**, peeled and cubed

1 unripe **papaya**, peeled and sliced

2 **tomatoes**, skinned and chopped

150 ml (¼ pint) **chicken stock**

150 ml (¼ pint) **coconut milk**

2 tablespoons **lime juice**

1 tablespoon **rum** or **Madeira**

salt and **pepper**

TO SERVE:

boiled **rice**

fried **bananas**

Caribbean curry

The chayote belongs to the same family as the cucumber and squash. If you can't find any, use butternut squash as a substitute.

1 Heat the oil in a heavy frying pan, add the chicken pieces and fry over a moderate heat until golden brown all over. Transfer to a flameproof casserole.

2 Add the onions, garlic and chilli to the frying pan and cook, stirring occasionally, over a moderate heat for about 5 minutes until the onions are soft. Add the curry powder, stir well and cook for 3 minutes, stirring. Add the aubergine, chayote, papaya and tomatoes, and cook for a further 2–3 minutes.

3 Put the curried mixture into the casserole and add the chicken stock and coconut milk. Cover and simmer for about 30 minutes, until the chicken is cooked and the vegetables are tender. Stir in the lime juice and rum or Madeira and season with salt and pepper. Serve with plain boiled rice and fried bananas.

PREP **10**

COOK **50**

SERVES **4–6**

fruity

Kashmiri chicken

Cardamom and cinnamon create a rich, warm aroma and flavour in this creamy dish.

1 Heat the ghee or vegetable oil in a deep frying pan. Add the onions, peppercorns, cardamoms and cinnamon and fry until the onions are golden. Add the ginger, garlic, chilli powder, paprika and salt to taste and fry, stirring occasionally, for 2 minutes.

2 Add the chicken pieces and fry until browned. Gradually add the yogurt, stirring constantly. Cover and cook gently for about 30 minutes.

50 g (2 oz) **ghee** or
2 tablespoons **vegetable oil**

3 large **onions**, finely sliced

10 **peppercorns**

10 **cardamoms**

5 cm (2 inch) piece of
cinnamon stick

5 cm (2 inch) piece of fresh
root ginger, peeled and
finely chopped

2 **garlic cloves**, finely
chopped

1 teaspoon **chilli powder**

2 teaspoons **paprika**

1.5 kg (3 lb) boneless,
skinless **chicken pieces**

250 ml (8 fl oz) **natural
yogurt**

salt

PREP
20

COOK
40

SERVES
6

creamy

3 tablespoons **vegetable oil**

2 **onions**, thinly sliced

8 long **green chillies**, thinly sliced lengthways

2.5 cm (1 inch) piece of fresh **root ginger**, peeled and thinly sliced

1 teaspoon **salt**

75 g (3 oz) **creamed coconut**, melted in 450 ml (¾ pint) hot **water**

4 skinless **chicken thighs** and 4 **chicken legs**

3 tablespoons **lime juice**

White chicken curry

This simple curry is quick to prepare and has just a few ingredients. It packs a punch though. Serve with steamed rice or grilled naan bread.

1 Heat the oil in a saucepan. Add the onions and fry gently for 3 minutes, but do not let them colour. Add the chillies, ginger and salt. Stir well, then pour in the coconut mixture.

2 Add the chicken and simmer gently for 30 minutes, or until cooked through. Stir occasionally and if there is any hint of the sauce catching, add a little water.

3 When ready, remove from the heat, stir in the lime juice and serve immediately.

PREP **5**

COOK **35**

SERVES **4**

hot

Phuket chicken curry

Phuket has become a popular tourist destination in recent years. This Thai island has many influences on its cuisine but here, plenty of traditional Thai ingredients are used.

1 Heat the oil in a large flameproof casserole, add the garlic and shallots and fry over a gentle heat, stirring constantly, for 3 minutes, or until just softened.

2 Add the lemon grass, lime leaves, curry paste, fish sauce and sugar to the pan. Fry for 1 minute, then add the stock and chicken drumsticks and bring the curry to the boil. Reduce the heat, cover and simmer gently, stirring occasionally, for 40–45 minutes, until the chicken is tender and cooked through.

3 Season to taste with salt and pepper and serve the curry garnished with chilli slices, lime leaves, if using, and lemon grass stalks. Serve with noodles or rice.

3 tablespoons **vegetable oil**

4 **garlic cloves**, crushed

3 **shallots**, chopped

3 **lemon grass stalks**, very finely chopped

6 **kaffir lime leaves**, shredded

3 tablespoons ready-made **green curry** paste

1 tablespoon **fish sauce**

2 teaspoons **palm sugar** or **soft brown sugar**

250 ml (8 fl oz) **chicken stock**

8 large **chicken drumsticks**

salt and **pepper**

TO GARNISH:

1 **red chilli**, sliced

kaffir lime leaves (optional)

lemon grass stalks

TO SERVE:

boiled **noodles** or **rice**

PREP
15

COOK
60

SERVES
4

piquant

4 tablespoons **groundnut oil**

625 g (1¼ lb) boneless, skinless **chicken breast**, cut into bite-sized pieces

1¼ teaspoons **chilli powder**

½ teaspoon **turmeric**

½ teaspoon **salt**

600 ml (1 pint) **coconut milk**

300 ml (½ pint) **chicken stock**

50 g (2 oz) **creamed coconut**, chopped

375 g (12 oz) **cellophane noodles**

a little **sesame oil**

salt

SPICE PASTE:

4 large **garlic cloves**, chopped

2 **onions**, chopped

1 large **red chilli**, deseeded and chopped

2.5 cm (1 inch) piece of fresh **root ginger**, peeled and chopped

1 teaspoon **shrimp paste**

continued opposite …

Chicken curry with noodles

This traditional Burmese dish is an ideal choice for an informal dinner party, as with its accompaniments it is a meal in itself.

1 Place all the spice paste ingredients in a blender or food processor and blend to a thick paste.

2 Heat the groundnut oil in a wok, add the spice paste and stir-fry over a low heat for 5 minutes, until softened.

3 Add the chicken pieces to the wok and stir-fry for a further 5 minutes to seal. Stir in the chilli powder, turmeric, salt, coconut milk and stock. Bring the curry to the boil, then reduce the heat and simmer very gently, stirring occasionally, for 15–20 minutes, or until the chicken pieces are tender.

4 Stir the creamed coconut into the curry and then simmer over a medium heat, stirring constantly, for 2–3 minutes, until the creamed coconut has dissolved and thickened the sauce slightly. Taste and adjust the seasoning if necessary.

PREP **30**   COOK **50**   SERVES **4**   **creamy**

TO SERVE:

3 **spring onions**, sliced

2 tablespoons **crispy fried shallots**

2 tablespoons **crispy fried garlic**

2 tablespoons **coriander leaves**

1 **lemon**, cut into wedges

whole **dried chillies**, fried (optional)

5 Drop the noodles into a pan of salted boiling water. Bring the water back to the boil and cook the noodles for 3 minutes, or according to the packet instructions. Drain the noodles and stir in a little sesame oil.

6 To serve, divide the noodles among 4 deep soup bowls and ladle some chicken curry over each portion. Serve the accompaniments separately.

Mussaman curry

500 g (1 lb) **chicken** or **beef**

2 tablespoons **vegetable oil**

2 **garlic cloves**, crushed

400 ml (14 fl oz) **coconut milk**

150 ml (¼ pint) **water**

2 tablespoons **fish sauce**

1 large **potato**, diced

1 **onion**, sliced lengthways

75 g (3 oz) **roasted peanuts**

1 tablespoon **soft brown sugar**

2 **kaffir lime leaves**, shredded

3 tablespoons **tamarind liquid** (see page 17)

MUSSAMAN CURRY PASTE:

6 large **dried red chillies**

1 tablespoon **ground coriander**

2 teaspoons **turmeric**

1 ground teaspoon each of **cinnamon**, **clove**, **star anise** and **cumin**

8 **cardamom pods**, bruised

1 teaspoon **coriander root**

5 cm (2 inch) **lemon grass**

4 **shallots**, chopped

2 teaspoons **shrimp paste**

8 **garlic cloves**, crushed

2.5 cm (1 inch) fresh **galangal**, peeled and chopped

4 **kaffir lime leaves**, shredded

1 teaspoon **salt**

A Thai curry is like a soup in consistency – watery but with plenty of flavour and chilli heat. This is one of the more mellow Thai curries, with plenty of galangal and turmeric to perfume the coconut sauce.

1 First make the curry paste. Heat a dry wok or frying pan until hot. Add all the dried spices and toast lightly. Remove from the heat. Chop the coriander root and lemon stalk then blend in a food processor, with the spices, shallots, shrimp paste and garlic. Add the galangal, kaffir lime leaves and salt and blend to a fine paste. Alternatively, pound the ingredients to a paste using a pestle and mortar.

2 Dice the meat and set aside. Heat the oil in a wok or heavy-based frying pan, add the garlic and fry for 1 minute or until softened and just turning golden brown. Add 2 tablespoons of the spice paste and, stirring constantly, fry for 2 minutes to cook the shallots.

3 Add the coconut milk and simmer gently to create a smooth sauce. Add the measured water and diced meat and simmer for 5 minutes. Add the fish sauce and potato and simmer for 10–15 minutes or until the meat has cooked through and the potato is tender but crisp.

4 Add the onion, peanuts, sugar, kaffir lime leaves and tamarind liquid and simmer for 1 minute then serve.

PREP **30** COOK **25** SERVES **4** mellow

Simple gurkha chicken

This is a version of a chicken dish regularly cooked by the Gurkha regiment at Sandhurst. Serve with plenty of boiled rice to soak up the juices.

1 Heat the oil in a saucepan and fry the chicken drumsticks until the skin is crisp. Remove the chicken from the pan and keep warm. Add the onions, garlic and ginger to the pan and fry until the onions are soft and golden.

2 Reduce the heat and add the cumin, turmeric, ground coriander, cayenne and 1 tablespoon of the water and cook, stirring, for 2 minutes. Add the tomatoes, yogurt and half of the chopped coriander. Increase the heat, return the chicken to the pan with the remaining water and bring to the boil.

3 Sprinkle the garam masala over the chicken, cover and simmer gently for 20 minutes. Season to taste. Just before serving add the salt and lemon juice and the remaining chopped coriander.

3 tablespoons **vegetable oil**

8 **chicken drumsticks**

2 **large onions**, finely chopped

4 **garlic cloves**, crushed

5 cm (2 inch) piece of fresh **root ginger**, peeled and finely chopped

1 teaspoon **ground cumin**

1 teaspoon **turmeric**

1 teaspoon **ground coriander**

1 teaspoon **cayenne pepper**

6 tablespoons **water**

250 g (8 oz) **tomatoes**, roughly chopped

150 ml (¼ pint) thick **Greek yogurt**

2 tablespoons chopped **coriander leaves**

1 tablespoon **garam masala**

½ teaspoon **salt**

juice of 1 **lemon**

PREP 10

COOK 35

SERVES 4

easy

2 tablespoons **groundnut oil**

300 ml (½ pint) **coconut milk**

150 ml (¼ pint) **water**

500 g (1 lb) **chicken, beef, pork** or **duck**, finely sliced

2–3 tablespoons **fish sauce**

150 g (5 oz) **Thai green aubergines**

1 tablespoon chopped **coriander leaves**

3 **lime leaves**, shredded

20 **holy basil leaves**

GREEN CURRY PASTE:

3 tablespoons **coriander leaves** and 4 **coriander roots**

4 **shallots**, chopped

3 **green chillies**, chopped

2 teaspoons **coriander seeds**

4 **garlic cloves**, crushed

1 teaspoon **shrimp paste**

2 **lemon grass stalks**, chopped

2.5 cm (1 inch) piece of fresh **galangal**, peeled and chopped

½ teaspoon **white peppercorns**

3 **kaffir lime leaves**, shredded

3 whole **cloves**

2 teaspoons **caster sugar**

2 tablespoons **fish sauce**

juice of 1 **lime**

88 chicken and duck

Green curry

Thai curries have a thin sauce and are traditionally served from a communal bowl. Thai table manners recommend adding only a tablespoon of food to a small mound of rice at any one time.

1 To make the green curry paste, place all the ingredients except the fish sauce and lime juice in a blender or food processor and blend to a semi-smooth paste. Add the fish sauce and lime juice and process to a smooth paste.

2 Heat the oil in a saucepan, add all of the green curry paste and fry for 2–3 minutes, stirring constantly. Add the coconut milk and measured water and bring the pan to a fast simmer.

3 Add the chicken or other meat to the curry sauce and simmer gently for 8–10 minutes. Add the fish sauce, to taste, the aubergines, chopped coriander and lime leaves. Simmer for a further 5 minutes. Stir in the basil leaves just before serving.

PREP **15**　COOK **20**　SERVES **4**　**hot**

Chicken shakuti

Shakuti is a Goanese speciality; it is rich and coconutty, with a sour tang from the lemon juice.

1 To make the spice mixture, spread the chillies, cumin, coriander seeds, fenugreek seeds, peppercorns and cloves over the surface of a baking sheet and roast in a preheated oven, 200°C (400°F), Gas Mark 6, for 5 minutes. Allow to cool slightly, then grind to a powder with the cardamom seeds and cinnamon. Add the turmeric.

2 Heat the oil in a saucepan and fry the onions and garlic until softened and beginning to brown. Add the spice mixture and toasted coconut and fry, stirring constantly, for 1 minute.

3 Add the chicken to the pan and seal in the oil. Add the peanuts, coconut milk and stock and simmer gently for 40 minutes.

4 Once the chicken has cooked through and is tender, add the lemon juice and salt. Simmer for 5 minutes, then serve.

3 tablespoons **vegetable oil**

2 **onions**, finely chopped

3 **garlic cloves**, crushed

50 g (2 oz) **desiccated coconut**, toasted

1.5 kg (3 lb) **chicken**, jointed

25 g (1 oz) **roasted peanuts**, roughly chopped

150 ml (¼ pint) **coconut milk**

150 ml (¼ pint) **chicken stock**

juice of 2 **lemons**

½ teaspoon **salt**

SPICE MIXTURE:

3 **dried Kashmiri chillies**

2 teaspoons **ground cumin**

1 tablespoon **coriander seeds**

1 teaspoon **fenugreek seeds**

½ teaspoon **peppercorns**

¼ teaspoon **cloves**

4 **cardamom pods**, seeds removed

1 small **cinnamon stick**

1 teaspoon **turmeric**

PREP **15**

COOK **60**

SERVES **4**

rich

2 tablespoons **groundnut oil**

2 **garlic cloves**, finely chopped

3 **shallots**, thinly sliced

3 **lemon grass stalks**, crushed and cut into 2.5 cm (1 inch) pieces

2 tablespoons **fish sauce**

½ teaspoon **pepper**

½ teaspoon **palm sugar** or **soft brown sugar**

1 teaspoon **spice paste** (see page 145) or **korma curry paste**

2 small **green chillies**, deseeded and chopped

750 g (1½ lb) boneless, skinless **chicken breasts**, cut into thin strips

3 tablespoons **chicken stock**

125 ml (4 fl oz) **coconut milk**

TO GARNISH:

2 tablespoons crushed **roasted peanuts**

handful of **coriander leaves**

Chicken and lemon grass curry

Lemon grass adds a subtle citrus flavour to dishes and complements many other flavours. Here, palm sugar is the sweet component of the dish and fish sauce adds the contrasting salty taste.

1 Heat the oil in a wok, add the garlic and shallots and stir-fry for 1 minute. Add the lemon grass, fish sauce, pepper, sugar, curry paste, chillies and chicken strips and stir-fry for 3–4 minutes.

2 Add the stock and coconut milk, mix well and simmer gently for 6 minutes, or until the chicken is cooked through. Serve the curry garnished with crushed peanuts and coriander leaves.

PREP
20

COOK
15

SERVES
4

citrus

Bangalore chicken curry

This 'green' curry from central southern India is made with a lot of coriander and green chillies.

1 Heat the ghee or oil in a large, heavy-based sauté pan. Add the onions and fry over a medium heat, stirring frequently, for about 5 minutes or until they are softened.

2 Stir in the garlic, turmeric and dhana jeera and cook, stirring, for a further 3 minutes.

3 Place the coriander leaves and green chillies in a blender or food processor and blend to a paste. Add this paste to the pan, reduce the heat to very low and cook, stirring constantly, for a further 10 minutes.

4 Add the chicken pieces to the pan, turn them in the spice mixture to coat them evenly, then add the stock, coconut milk and salt. Bring to the boil, then reduce the heat, cover and simmer, stirring and turning the chicken occasionally, for about 50 minutes or until the juices from the chicken run clear when tested with a skewer. Stir in the lemon juice and taste and adjust the amout of salt if necessary.

5 Transfer the cooked chicken pieces to a serving dish and keep them warm. Increase the heat and boil the curry sauce for 5–8 minutes to thicken it. Pour it over the chicken.

PREP **20**

COOK **80**

SERVES **6**

fresh

3 tablespoons **ghee** or **vegetable oil**

2 onions, thinly sliced

6 **garlic cloves**, chopped

1 teaspoon **turmeric**

1½ teaspoons **dhana jeera powder** (see page 17)

40 g (1½ oz) **coriander leaves**

3 large **green chillies**, deseeded and chopped

1.75 kg (3½ lb) **chicken**, cut into 8 pieces

150 ml (¼ pint) **chicken stock**

300 ml (½ pint) **coconut milk**

1 teaspoon **salt**

1 tablespoon **lemon juice**

2 tablespoons **vegetable oil**

400 g (13 oz) boneless, skinless **chicken breast**, cut into strips

250 ml (8 fl oz) **chicken stock**

salt and **pepper**

SPICE PASTE:

1 **onion**, roughly chopped

6 **green chillies**, deseeded and chopped

6 **garlic cloves**, chopped

2 teaspoons peeled and grated fresh **root ginger**

1 tablespoon **ground coriander**

2 teaspoons **ground cumin**

large bunch of **coriander leaves**, roughly chopped

150 ml (¼ pint) **water**

Bombay chicken masala

This is an excellent dish for a family supper or a mid-week meal with friends.

1 Place the spice paste ingredients in a blender or food processor and blend to a fairly smooth paste. Set aside.

2 Heat the oil in a large nonstick frying pan and add the spice paste. Fry, stirring constantly, for 1 minute, then add the chicken. Fry, stirring, for 2–3 minutes, then add the stock. Mix well, cover and cook gently for 10–12 minutes, or until the chicken is tender. Season with salt and pepper and serve hot.

PREP
10

COOK
15

SERVES
4

spicy

Thai chicken curry

The lemon grass and kaffir lime leaves give this dish a really light, fresh flavour. Serve with basmati rice.

1 Heat the oil in a saucepan, add the lemon grass, lime leaves, chilli, ginger, onion and garlic and fry for 2 minutes. Add the red and green peppers and chopped chicken and fry for 5 minutes.

2 Pour in the coconut milk and the stock and simmer for 10 minutes, or until the chicken is cooked through.

3 Stir in the coriander leaves and season to taste with salt and pepper.

1 tablespoon **sunflower oil**

1 **lemon grass stalk**, cut into 4 pieces

2 **kaffir lime leaves**, halved

1–2 **red chillies**, finely chopped

2.5 cm (1 inch) piece of fresh **root ginger**, peeled and grated

1 **onion**, finely chopped

1 **garlic clove**, crushed

1 **red pepper**, cored, deseeded and chopped

1 **green pepper**, cored, deseeded and chopped

3 boneless, skinless **chicken breasts**, chopped

400 ml (14 fl oz) can **coconut milk**

150 ml (¼ pint) **chicken stock**

2 tablespoons chopped **coriander leaves**

salt and **pepper**

PREP
15

COOK
20

SERVES
4

fresh

1 tablespoon **vegetable oil**

1½ tablespoons **green curry paste** (see page 15)

4 tablespoons **coconut milk**

125 g (4 oz) boneless, skinless **chicken breast**, cut into bite-sized pieces

2 **lime leaves**, torn, or 2 strips of **lime rind**

½ **lemon grass stalk**, cut in fine, diagonal slices (optional)

50 g (2 oz) **bamboo shoots**

3 small **green aubergines**, or 1 **purple aubergine**, chopped

50 g (2 oz) **courgettes**, cut in diagonal chunks

1 large **red chilli**, diagonally sliced

6 tablespoons **chicken stock**

1 tablespoon **palm sugar** or **soft brown sugar**

3 tablespoons **fish sauce** or **light soy sauce**

TO GARNISH:

sprigs of **sweet basil**

Green curry chicken

A classic Thai recipe, this version is extremely quick and easy to prepare. Make sure you have all the ingredients to hand before you begin cooking.

1   Heat the oil in a wok and stir in the curry paste. Heat through for 30 seconds, then add the coconut milk and cook, stirring, for 1 minute.

2   Add the chicken, bring up to a simmer and add all the remaining ingredients. Simmer for 10 minutes, stirring occasionally.

3   Transfer the curry to a warmed serving bowl, garnish with basil sprigs and serve.

PREP
7

COOK
15

SERVES
2

hearty

Chicken and coconut curry

Chicken and coconut milk work very well together and the potatoes add a hearty finish to this robust dish.

1 Heat the oil in a large saucepan. Add the chicken drumsticks and brown on all sides. Stir the coconut milk into the pan and bring to the boil. Add the curry paste. Lower the heat and simmer for 2 hours.

2 Stir in the potatoes, onion, lemon juice, fish sauce, sugar and peanuts, cover the pan and simmer for a further 20 minutes. Serve immediately.

3 tablespoons **vegetable oil**

4 **chicken drumsticks**

350 ml (12 fl oz) **coconut milk**

4½ teaspoons **mussaman curry paste** (see page 86)

4 **new potatoes**, scrubbed or peeled

1 **onion**, quartered

¼ teaspoon **lemon juice**

4½ teaspoons **fish sauce**

1½ teaspoons **sugar**

25 g (1 oz) **roasted peanuts**

PREP
15

COOK
150

SERVES
4

creamy

1 **onion**, chopped

4 **garlic cloves**, crushed

15 g (½ oz) **mint leaves**

1 tablespoon peeled and grated fresh **root ginger**

3 tablespoons **ghee**

½ teaspoon **saffron threads**, infused in 2 tablespoons boiling **water** for 10 minutes

2 teaspoons **garam masala**

1 teaspoon **chilli powder**

750 g (1½ lb) boneless, skinless **chicken breasts**

½ teaspoon **salt**

100 ml (3½ fl oz) **natural yogurt**

175 g (6 oz) **tomatoes**, chopped

TO GARNISH:

sprigs of **mint**

Chicken yogurt curry with mint

Yogurt and mint is a classic combination and it is often used to complement more spicy, robust ingredients. In this chicken recipe it works with the chilli to create a spicy yet cool flavour.

1 Place the onion, garlic, mint leaves and ginger in a blender or food processor and blend to a smooth paste.

2 Heat the ghee in a large, heavy-based pan, add the blended paste and fry gently for 5 minutes.

3 Add the saffron with its infused water, the garam masala and chilli powder and fry for a further 1 minute.

4 Cut each chicken breast into 3 pieces and add the pieces to the pan with the salt. Stir to coat the chicken thoroughly in the spice mixture and cook for a further 5 minutes, to seal the chicken.

5 Add the yogurt and tomatoes and stir well. Cover the pan and simmer gently for 15 minutes, until the chicken is cooked through.

6 Remove the lid and simmer uncovered for 45 minutes more to thicken the sauce slightly. Taste the sauce and adjust the amount of salt, if necessary.

7 Transfer the curry to a warmed serving dish and garnish with mint sprigs.

PREP **20**

COOK **70**

SERVES **4–6**

spicy

Duck vindaloo

This is a traditional hot and sour curry that originates from the former Portuguese colony of Goa. The vinegar in the recipe acts as a pickling agent, enabling this curry to be made a few days in advance, if you wish.

1 Slice the duck breasts diagonally into 2.5 cm (1 inch) thick slices and place them in a shallow, non-metallic dish.

2 Place the chillies, vinegar, garlic, ginger, mustard seeds and peppercorns in a blender or food processor and blend to a smooth paste. Stir the ground coriander, cumin and turmeric into the paste.

3 Pour the mixture over the duck slices and mix until evenly coated. Cover and leave to marinate for 3 hours at room temperature or overnight in the refrigerator.

4 Heat the oil in a heavy-based saucepan. Remove the duck from the marinade, reserving the marinade, and add the duck to the pan with the salt. Cook over a gentle heat for 5 minutes, then pour away any excess fat from the pan.

5 Add the marinade with the measured water and stir well. Cover and simmer, stirring, for 30 minutes, or until the duck is tender. Stir in the sugar, increase the heat and cook the curry over a medium-high heat for 6–8 minutes, stirring frequently. The sauce should be of a thick, coating consistency. Serve hot.

PREP **15***

COOK **45**

SERVES **4**

hot

* plus at least
3 hours marinating

750 g (1½ lb) boneless **duck breasts**

1 tablespoon **vegetable oil**

1 teaspoon **salt**

150 ml (¼ pint) **water**

1 tablespoon **palm sugar** or **soft brown sugar**

SPICE PASTE:

6 **dried red chillies**, deseeded and chopped

150 ml (¼ pint) **malt vinegar**

6 **garlic cloves**, chopped

2.5 cm (1 inch) piece of fresh **root ginger**, peeled and grated

1 teaspoon **mustard seeds**, lightly crushed

20 **black peppercorns**, lightly crushed

1 tablespoon **ground coriander**

1 tablespoon **ground cumin**

1 teaspoon **turmeric**

Duck padre curry

4 **duck legs**, about 175 g (6 oz) each

1 large **onion**, chopped

4 **garlic cloves**, finely chopped

1 tablespoon peeled and grated fresh **root ginger**

1 **lemon grass stalk**, halved lengthways

4 **curry leaves**

½ teaspoon **ground cinnamon**

1 teaspoon **salt**

50 ml (2 fl oz) **malt vinegar**

300 ml (½ pint) **coconut milk**

50 ml (2 fl oz) **whisky**

2 teaspoons **palm sugar** or **soft brown sugar** or according to taste

SPICE MIXTURE:

6 **dried red chillies**

2 teaspoons **cumin seeds**

2 teaspoons **coriander seeds**

The origins of this Sri Lankan curry's name remain a mystery. One suggestion is that the recipe's use of whisky might allow a seemingly abstemious vicar a surreptitious tot (or sip) of his favourite tipple!

1 Trim away any excess fat from the duck legs and place the duck in a large, heavy-based saucepan. Add the onion, garlic, ginger, lemon grass, curry leaves, cinnamon, salt, vinegar and coconut milk, and stir to mix all the ingredients.

2 Dry-fry the ingredients for the spice mix in a small frying pan for 2 minutes until fragrant, then grind them to a powder in a spice mill or with a pestle and mortar.

3 Stir the ground spices into the pan with the duck, bring the curry to the boil, then reduce the heat, cover and simmer gently for 1 hour, stirring occasionally, until the duck is tender. After 1 hour, remove the lid and cook the curry uncovered for a further 15 minutes.

4 Stir the whisky and sugar into the curry and simmer it for a further 15 minutes. Taste and adjust the seasoning if necessary and serve immediately.

PREP
10

COOK
105

SERVES
4

spicy

Balinese duck curry

Duck is a robust meat and its high fat content will add plenty of flavour to this dish. It can handle big flavours and the spice paste is perfect.

1 Place the spice paste ingredients in a blender or food processor and blend to a thick paste.

2 Heat the vegetable oil in a wide sauté pan, add the paste and fry over a gentle heat, stirring constantly, for about 3 minutes or until softened and fragrant.

3 Add the duck portions, lemon grass, lime leaves and salt to the pan. Stir to coat the duck evenly in the spice mixture and fry for a further 4 minutes to seal the meat.

4 Add the measured water to the pan, stir well and bring to the boil. Reduce the heat, cover the pan and cook the curry gently, stirring occasionally, for 45 minutes, until the duck is tender.

5 Uncover the pan, stir in the sugar and increase the heat to moderate. Cook the curry, stirring frequently, for a further 30 minutes, until the duck is cooked and the sauce is thick. Garnish with the sliced chillies and serve.

4 tablespoons **vegetable oil**

1.5 kg (3 lb) oven-ready **duck**, cut into 4 portions

1 **lemon grass stalk**, halved lengthways

4 **kaffir lime leaves**, bruised

1 teaspoon **salt**

300 ml (½ pint) **water**

2 teaspoons **palm sugar** or **soft brown sugar**

SPICE PASTE:

8 **shallots**, chopped

4 **garlic cloves**, chopped

6 large **green chillies**, deseeded and chopped

5 cm (2 inch) piece of fresh **root ginger**, peeled and chopped

2.5 cm (1 inch) piece of fresh **galangal**, peeled and chopped

2 teaspoons **turmeric**

¼ teaspoon **pepper**

6 **candlenuts** or **macadamia nuts** (optional)

TO GARNISH:

2 **green chillies**, sliced

PREP **25**

COOK **90**

SERVES **4**

robust

2–2.5 kg (4–5 lb) oven-ready **duck** with giblets

coarse **salt**, for sprinkling

500 ml (17 fl oz) **thick coconut milk** (see page 15)

4 **kaffir lime leaves**, plus extra to garnish

7½ teaspoons **green curry paste** (see page 15)

500 ml (17 fl oz) **thin coconut milk** (see page 15)

2–3 **green chillies**, deseeded and sliced

fish sauce, to taste

Green duck curry

This is a variation of green chicken curry and the sauce here will be richer for the addition of duck.

1 Sprinkle the skin of the duck generously with coarse salt. Set aside for 15 minutes.

2 Brush off the salt and chop the duck into 5 cm (2 inch) pieces. Heat a wok or frying pan over a medium-high heat. Add a few pieces of duck and brown thoroughly. Remove and drain on kitchen paper. Brown the remaining duck in the same way. Discard the fat and wipe the wok clean.

3 Reduce the heat to moderate. Skim the coconut cream from the top of the thick coconut milk and bring to the boil in the wok, then add the lime leaves and curry paste. Reduce the heat and cook, stirring constantly, until the oil begins to separate. Add the duck pieces, turn to cover evenly with the sauce, then cook gently for 5 minutes.

4 Add both the coconut milks, bring just to the boil, then reduce the heat. Simmer, stirring occasionally, for 1–1¼ hours until tender. Remove from the heat, transfer to a bowl and allow to cool. Cover and chill overnight.

5 Skim excess fat from the curry, return to the wok and stir in the chillies. Simmer until heated through and serve.

PREP **15***

COOK **105**

SERVES **4–6**

rich

* plus 15 minutes standing and overnight chilling

Red duck curry

Another variation of the classic chicken dish. This recipe uses red curry paste and the fat from the duck will add to the flavour.

1 Take the skin and meat off the duck, chop it into bite-sized pieces and set aside.

2 Heat the oil in a wok, add the red curry paste and fry, stirring, for 30 seconds. Add 3 tablespoons of the coconut milk, mix it with the paste, then add the remainder and stir over a gentle heat for 1 minute.

3 Add the duck and stir for 2 minutes. Add the sugar, lime leaves, peas, chilli, chicken stock, tomatoes and pineapple. Mix well together and finally, with the curry simmering, add the fish sauce. Give it all a good stir and transfer the contents of the wok into a bowl. Serve with the extra pineapple and noodles, if liked, and garnished with red pepper and spring onion strips.

¼ roast **duck**

1 tablespoon **oil**

1½ tablespoons **red curry paste** (see page 16)

150 ml (¼ pint) **coconut milk**

1 tablespoon **palm sugar** or **soft brown sugar**

3 **kaffir lime leaves**, torn, or ¼ teaspoon grated **lime rind**

65 g (2½ oz) **peas**

1 large **red chilli**, diagonally sliced

4 tablespoons **chicken stock**

2 **tomatoes**, finely diced

125 g (4 oz) fresh or tinned **pineapple**, cut into chunks, plus extra to serve

1 tablespoon **fish sauce**

TO GARNISH:

red pepper strips

spring onion strips

noodles, to serve

PREP
15

COOK
5

SERVES
3–4

robust

fish and shellfish

3 tablespoons **vegetable oil**

1 **onion**, sliced

2 **garlic cloves**, crushed

1 tablespoon peeled and grated fresh **root ginger**

1 teaspoon **black mustard seeds**

6 **dried curry leaves**

2 tablespoons **curry paste for seafood**

300 ml (½ pint) **coconut milk**

½ teaspoon **salt**

3 small **tomatoes**, cut into wedges

475 g (15 oz) can of **sardines in tomato sauce**

TO GARNISH:

2 **green chillies**, sliced

2 tablespoons **coriander leaves**

Malaysian sardine curry

This is a popular store-cupboard curry in Malaysia; it uses canned sardines, but for a different curry you could replace the sardines with canned salmon.

1 Heat the oil in a saucepan, add the onion, garlic and ginger and fry over a gentle heat, stirring frequently for about 4 minutes or until softened but not coloured. Add the mustard seeds and curry leaves and cook for a further 2 minutes.

2 Stir in the curry paste and cook, stirring, for 2 minutes, then add the coconut milk and salt, stir well and simmer the sauce for 5 minutes until it has thickened slightly.

3 Add the tomatoes, then cover the pan and cook the curry for a further 5 minutes. Break the sardines into large chunks and add them to the pan with the sauce from the can. Simmer the curry gently for a further 3 minutes. Taste and adjust the amount of salt if necessary, then serve garnished with sliced green chillies and coriander leaves.

PREP **5**   COOK **25**   SERVES **4**   **creamy**

Fish mollee

This mild Anglo-Indian curry is wonderful served with boiled rice, lime pickle and poppadoms. Vary the recipe by substituting raw tiger prawns for the fish, cooking them until the prawns have just turned pink.

1 Place the fish in a large, shallow, non-metallic dish and sprinkle with salt and the lemon juice. Cover and set aside.

2 Heat the oil in a large nonstick frying pan and add the onion and garlic. Fry, stirring constantly, for 2–3 minutes and then add the turmeric, chillies and coconut milk. Cook briskly for 2–3 minutes.

3 Add the fish. Stir carefully and add the vinegar. Cover the pan and cook for 7–10 minutes, or until the fish is cooked through. Season with salt and pepper to taste and serve hot.

875 g (1¾ lb) thick, skinless **cod** or **halibut fillets**, cut into 4cm (1½ inch) pieces

4 tablespoons **lemon juice**

1 tablespoon **vegetable oil**

1 **onion**, finely chopped

3 **garlic cloves**, crushed

1 teaspoon **turmeric**

4 **green chillies**, deseeded and finely chopped

300 ml (½ pint) **coconut milk**

1 tablespoon **white wine vinegar**

salt and **pepper**

PREP
10

COOK
15

SERVES
4

mild

2 tablespoons **vegetable oil**

1 **onion**, finely chopped

4 **garlic cloves**, sliced

1 teaspoon peeled and
grated fresh **root ginger**

½ teaspoon **turmeric**

1 teaspoon **chilli powder**

1 teaspoon **ground cumin**

2 teaspoons **ground
coriander**

1 teaspoon **garam masala**

500 g (1 lb) thick **white fish
fillets**, cut into 2.5 cm
(1 inch) pieces

400 g (13 oz) can **chopped
tomatoes**

2 teaspoons **sea salt**

2 teaspoons **sugar**

Tomato fish curry

Any firm white fish, such as cod or haddock, is suitable for
this fresh, aromatic curry.

1 Heat the oil in a large nonstick frying pan and fry the
onion until soft and lightly browned. Add the garlic,
ginger, turmeric, chilli powder, cumin, coriander and
garam masala and fry for 30 seconds.

2 Add the fish and stir gently for 1 minute.

3 Add the tomatoes, salt and sugar, stir carefully, cover
and simmer gently for 7–10 minutes, or until the fish is
cooked through. Serve hot.

PREP
10

COOK
15

SERVES
4

fresh

Shellfish curry

Shellfish are fantastic when cooked in a sauce and these large prawns should really soak up the flavours of this delicious dish.

1 Place the spice paste ingredients in a blender or food processor and blend to a smooth paste.

2 Next, heat the oil in a large wok and stir-fry the garlic, shallots and chillies for 2–3 minutes. Add the spice paste and continue to stir-fry for 3 minutes, then add the coconut milk, fish sauce and lime leaves. Mix well and simmer for 5 minutes.

3 Finally, add the prawns, stirring, and then the mussels. Cover the curry and simmer for a few minutes, until all the mussels are open. Discard any mussels which have not opened before serving.

PREP 15 · COOK 15 · SERVES 4 · hot

1 tablespoon **vegetable oil**

4 large **garlic cloves**, crushed and finely chopped

4 **shallots**, finely chopped

2 small **red chillies**, finely chopped

600 ml (1 pint) **coconut milk**

1 tablespoon **Vietnamese fish sauce**

6 **kaffir lime leaves**

375 g (12 oz) large **raw prawns**, peeled and deveined

1 kg (2 lb) **mussels**, scrubbed and debearded

SPICE PASTE:

1 heaped teaspoon **Thai yellow curry paste** (see page 147)

2 teaspoons **cumin seeds**, toasted and ground

1 teaspoon **turmeric**

1 teaspoon **ground coriander**

1 **lemon grass stalk**, finely sliced

1 teaspoon **palm sugar** or **soft brown sugar**

5 ripe **tomatoes**, chopped

750 g (1½ lb) skinless **cod fillets**, cut into 10 cm (4 inch) pieces

1 teaspoon **turmeric**

½ teaspoon **salt**

1 quantity **tamarind liquid** (see page 17) made with 1 tablespoon pulp soaked in 300ml (½ pint) water

4 tablespoons **groundnut oil**

8 **curry leaves**

2 teaspoons **onion seeds**

2 **onions**, thinly sliced

2 large **green chillies**, deseeded and thinly sliced

2 tablespoons **Madras curry paste**

4 small **tomatoes**, quartered

4 tablespoons **chopped coriander leaves**

Madras fish curry

This hot curry has the added tartness of tamarind – a favourite ingredient in Indian fish curries.

1 Rub the cod fillet with the turmeric and salt, and place in a shallow, non-metallic dish.

2 Next, pour the tamarind liquid over the fish. Cover and marinate for 1 hour in the refrigerator.

3 Meanwhile, prepare the curry sauce. Heat the oil in a heavy-based sauté pan, add the curry leaves and onion seeds and cook gently for 1 minute.

4 Stir in the sliced onions and chillies and cook for 3 minutes until soft but not coloured. Stir in the curry paste and cook for a further 2 minutes.

5 Remove the fish from the tamarind liquid and set aside. Add the tamarind liquid to the pan of fried ingredients with the tomatoes. Stir gently to mix, then simmer the curry sauce gently for 10 minutes.

6 Add the fish and chopped coriander to the pan, cover and cook for 8 minutes or until the fish is just cooked through. Taste and adjust the seasoning if necessary.

PREP **15***   COOK **25**   SERVES **4**   **hot**

* plus 1 hour marinating

Assam fish curry

This richly flavoured dish uses tamarind liquid, chillies and palm sugar in the sauce. The fish needs to be robust and meaty so it doesn't break up too much in the pan.

1 Place the spice paste ingredients in a blender or food processor and blend to a thick paste. Heat the oil in a large saucepan, add the spice paste and fry over a gentle heat, stirring constantly, for about 5 minutes until softened.

2 Add the tamarind liquid to the pan with the tomatoes, aubergines and chillies. Bring to the boil, then reduce the heat, cover the pan and simmer gently for 12 minutes.

3 Add the sugar, salt and fish to the pan and stir gently to coat the fish in the sauce. Cover and cook the curry over a gentle heat for a further 7 minutes, or until the fish is cooked through. Before serving, taste and adjust the seasoning if necessary.

4 tablespoons **vegetable oil**

1 quantity **tamarind liquid** (see page 17), made with 3 tablespoons pulp soaked in 250 ml (8 fl oz) boiling water

2 **tomatoes**, quartered

2 **baby aubergines**, weighing about 50 g (2 oz) each, quartered

2 large **red chillies**, quartered lengthways and deseeded

1 tablespoon **palm sugar** or **soft brown sugar**

½ teaspoon **salt**

625 g (1¼ lb) skinless **haddock** or **halibut**, cut into 5 cm (2 inch) pieces

SPICE PASTE:

5 small **dried chillies** soaked in cold water for 10 minutes, then deseeded and chopped

8 **shallots**, chopped

3 **lemon grass stalks**, chopped

2 **red chillies**, deseeded and chopped

2.5 cm (1 inch) piece of fresh **galangal**, chopped

2 teaspoons **dried shrimp paste**

1 teaspoon **turmeric**

PREP **20**　COOK **30**　SERVES **4**　hot

Malabar fish curry

1 tablespoon **chilli powder**

1 teaspoon **turmeric**

½ teaspoon **yellow mustard seeds**

½ teaspoon **ground cinnamon**

4 large **garlic cloves**, crushed

750 g (1½ lb) **swordfish, tuna, shark** or **haddock**, cut into thick steaks

125 g (4 oz) raw **tiger prawns**, peeled and deveined

2 tablespoons **vegetable oil**

2.5 cm (1 inch) piece of fresh **root ginger**, peeled and finely chopped

2 **green chillies**, finely chopped

2 **onions**, finely chopped

10–15 **curry leaves**

450 ml (¾ pint) **coconut milk**

150 ml (¼ pint) **fish stock** or **water**

salt and **pepper**

TO GARNISH:

2 tablespoons finely chopped **coriander leaves**

TO SERVE:

chapattis

On the south-west coast of India, south of Goa, is the Malabar coast, which has a wealth of produce including home-grown spices, coconuts and, of course, plenty of fish. The chilli and the coconut are vital to this region's cooking.

1 Mix the chilli powder, turmeric, mustard seeds, cinnamon and garlic and rub into the fish and prawns. Place in a non-metallic dish, cover and leave to marinate in the refrigerator for 2 hours.

2 Heat the oil in a pan and fry the ginger, chillies and onions for 5 minutes to soften and slightly brown. Add the pieces of marinated fish and fry lightly on both sides. Add any remaining spice mixture together with the curry leaves, then stir in the coconut milk and stock and simmer very gently for 8 minutes.

3 Add the marinated prawns to the pan and simmer for a further 5 minutes. Season to taste with salt and pepper and garnish with chopped coriander. Serve with chapattis.

PREP
10*

COOK
25

SERVES
4–6

fresh

* plus 2 hours marinating

Fish masala with coconut sambal

Coconut-fried fish with a spicy hot sambal is an everyday dish in Malaysia and India. The fish is rubbed with a spice mix, then quickly fried in coconut (palm) oil until crisp and golden brown.

1 Remove the scales from the fish, then fillet and chop them into 7.5 cm (3 inch) pieces. Mix the chilli, turmeric and salt and rub into the fish on all sides. Set aside for 1 hour to marinate.

2 To make the sambal, mix the measured water into the desiccated coconut to moisten and set aside. Put all the remaining sambal ingredients into a blender and blend to a smooth paste. Mix the paste into the moistened coconut, then transfer to a small bowl.

3 Heat the oil until hot and fry the fish for 3 minutes on each side until well cooked, golden brown and very crisp. Remove with a slotted spoon and drain on kitchen paper.

4 Serve the warm fish on banana leaves with the coconut sambal, plain boiled rice and lime pickle (optional). Eat with your fingers.

4 small **pomfret, mackerel, snapper** or **bream**, gutted

1 teaspoon **ground chilli**

¼ teaspoon **turmeric**

½ teaspoon **salt**

4 tablespoons **coconut** or **vegetable oil**

COCONUT SAMBAL:

3 tablespoons boiling **water**

50 g (2 oz) **desiccated coconut**

½ teaspoon **chilli powder**

1 teaspoon **ground fish powder** or **ground shrimp**

3 **curry leaves**

1 piece of **pandanus leaf** (optional)

⅓ **onion**, finely chopped

1 teaspoon **lemon juice**

TO SERVE:

banana leaves

boiled **rice**

lime pickle

PREP
15*

COOK
10

* plus 1 hour
marinating

SERVES
4

spicy

500 g (1 lb) fish such as **tuna, swordfish, mackerel, pomfret** or **haddock**, skin and bones removed, and roughly cubed

3 tablespoons **groundnut** or **vegetable oil**

2 **onions**, finely chopped

4 **garlic cloves**, crushed

1 **lemon grass stalk**, bruised

2.5 cm (1 inch) piece of fresh **root ginger**, peeled and finely chopped

2 teaspoons **turmeric**

6–8 **curry leaves**

400 g (13 oz) can **plum tomatoes**

150 ml (¼ pint) **fish stock** or **water**

300 ml (½ pint) **coconut milk**

175 g (6 oz) raw **tiger prawns**, peeled and deveined

meat from 1 small cooked **crab** (see page 15)

salt and **pepper**

continued opposite …

Sri Lankan seafood curry

Seafood curry is a great favourite of Sri Lankans. The spice mixture is a variation on Rani King and Chandra Khan's recipe. Any remainder can be kept in an airtight container, it should be used within 1 month for the freshest flavour.

1 First prepare the spice mixture. Spread all the spices on one baking sheet and the rice on a separate sheet and roast in a preheated oven, 200°C (400°F), Gas Mark 6, for 5–6 minutes or until toasted. The rice will take slightly longer than the spices. Stir occasionally to toast them evenly. Take care that the spices do not burn. Leave to cool, then grind the spices and the toasted rice to a powder.

2 Rub 2 tablespoons of the spice mixture into the fish. Cover and set aside for 30 minutes to marinate.

PREP **20***

COOK **75**

SERVES **4**

piquant

* plus 30 minutes marinating

3 Heat 2 tablespoons of the oil in a saucepan and gently fry the onions for 20 minutes or until soft and golden brown. Add the garlic, bruised lemon grass, ginger, turmeric and curry leaves and cook for 2–3 minutes. Add the tomatoes, stock and coconut milk to the pan and simmer gently, stirring occasionally, for 15 minutes. Increase the heat and boil, stirring, for 10 minutes to thicken the sauce slightly. Season the sauce to taste with salt and pepper.

4 Heat the remaining oil in a frying pan and sear the fish on all sides. Add to the tomato sauce with the tiger prawns and crab meat and simmer gently for 6–7 minutes. Season to taste. Remove the pan from the heat and leave to stand, covered, for 8 minutes for the fish to finish cooking in the curry's residual heat before serving.

SRI LANKAN SPICE MIXTURE:

2 teaspoons **coriander seeds**

1 teaspoon **cumin seeds**

3 **dried red chillies**

1 teaspoon **fennel seeds**

¼ teaspoon **fenugreek seeds**

5 cm (2 inch) piece of **cinnamon stick**

½ teaspoon whole **cloves**

3 **cardamom pods**, seeds removed

1 teaspoon **black peppercorns**

1 teaspoon **yellow mustard seeds**

1 tablespoon **basmati rice**

4 thick **halibut steaks** or **fillets**, each about 250 g (8 oz)

2 tablespoons **medium curry paste**

juice of 2 **limes**

salt and **pepper**

Baked halibut masala

Nothing could be simpler than coating halibut steaks or fillets in a ready-made curry paste mixed with lime juice, then baking them until just cooked through. Serve with steamed rice and a simple vegetable.

1 Line a large baking sheet with nonstick baking paper. Mix together the curry paste and lime juice. Season, and spread this mixture over the fish.

2 Put the fish on the prepared baking sheet and bake in a preheated oven, 200°C (400°F), Gas Mark 6, for 15–20 minutes or until the fish is cooked through. Remove from the oven and serve immediately.

PREP
5

COOK
20

SERVES
4

citrus

Salmon and tamarind curry

Tamarind adds a lovely sharp tang to this curry, and helps to cut through the richness of the salmon and coconut milk and enhance the flavours of the spices. If you can't find it, use the juice of a lemon or lime instead.

1 Heat the oil in a large, nonstick wok or frying pan. When it is hot, add the garlic, cumin seeds, black onion seeds, mustard seeds and coriander seeds. Stir-fry for 1–2 minutes, then add the curry leaves and the salmon. Stir-fry over a high heat for 5–6 minutes.

2 In a bowl, mix together the remaining ingredients and pour into the fish mixture. Turn the heat down to medium and allow to simmer for 3–4 minutes, stirring often, until the salmon is cooked through. Season well and serve immediately, garnished with coriander leaves and a few black onion seeds. Accompany with pilau or steamed basmati rice.

2 tablespoons **sunflower oil**

2 **garlic cloves**, thinly sliced

2 teaspoons **cumin seeds**

1 teaspoon **black onion seeds**, pus extra to garnish

1 teaspoon **black mustard seeds**

1 teaspoon crushed **coriander seeds**

10–12 **curry leaves**

750 g (1½ lb) **salmon fillet**, cut into bite-sized pieces

2 tablespoons **tomato purée**

½ teaspoon **caster sugar**

1 teaspoon **garam masala**

1 teaspoon **ground cumin**

6 tablespoons finely chopped **coriander leaves**, plus extra leaves to garnish

1 **red chilli**, finely sliced

1 teaspoon **tamarind paste**

250 ml (8 fl oz) **coconut milk**

salt

TO SERVE:

pilau or steamed **basmati rice**

PREP
10

COOK
15

SERVES
4

spicy

750 g (1½ lb) thick **cod fillet**, skinned and cut into bite-sized cubes

2 tablespoons **plain flour**

2 tablespoons light **olive oil**

1 **onion**, halved and thinly sliced

2 **garlic cloves**, crushed

1 teaspoon **turmeric**

1 **green chilli**, finely chopped

2 tablespoons **lemon juice**

200 ml (7 fl oz) half-fat **coconut milk**

100 ml (3½ fl oz) very low-fat **natural fromage frais**

Creamy fish korma

Delicately flavoured korma curries are usually enriched with cream and ground almonds, but here half-fat coconut milk and very low-fat fromage frais are used instead. Serve with a fresh vegetable accompaniment and plain boiled rice.

1 Lightly coat the fish with flour, patting away any excess. Heat the oil in a large, nonstick frying pan over a medium heat and add the fish. Fry the fish for 2–3 minutes on each side. Remove from the pan with a slotted spoon and set aside.

2 Add the onion to the pan and stir-fry over a medium heat for 5–6 minutes. Add the garlic, turmeric, chilli and lemon juice and stir and fry for another 2–3 minutes. Stir in the coconut milk, bring to the boil and then reduce the heat and stir and simmer gently for 8–10 minutes.

3 Return the fish to the pan, spoon the sauce over the fish and cook for 4–5 minutes until heated through. Remove from the heat and stir in the fromage frais before serving.

PREP **10**

COOK **30**

SERVES **4**

creamy

Fish tandoori

It's important to allow the fish to marinate in the spices for a long time as it will absorb the flavours more thoroughly. The yogurt helps to bind the spices together without dissolving any of the pungent flavours.

1 First, make the tandoori marinade. Put the yogurt in a non-metallic bowl with the oil, paprika, cumin, fennel seeds, chilli powder and a little salt. Mix well together.

2 Place the halibut steaks in the bowl and rub well with the tandoori mixture. Cover the bowl and leave in a cool place to marinate for 4–5 hours.

3 Transfer the marinated fish to a shallow, ovenproof dish. Bake uncovered in a preheated oven, 180°C (350°F), Gas Mark 4, for 20–25 minutes.

4 Arrange the lettuce on a warmed serving dish and place the fish on top. Spoon over the juices and serve garnished with fennel and lemon wedges.

4 x 175 g (6 oz) **halibut steaks**

TANDOORI MARINADE

50 ml (2 fl oz) **natural yogurt**

2 tablespoons **vegetable oil**

2 tablespoons **paprika**

1 tablespoon **ground cumin**

1 teaspoon **ground fennel seeds**

1 teaspoon **chilli powder**

salt

TO GARNISH:

1 small **lettuce**, shredded

1 **fennel bulb**, sliced

wedges of **lemon**

PREP
15*

COOK
25

SERVES
4

spicy

* plus 4–5 hours marinating

4 tablespoons **olive oil**

1 teaspoon **mustard seeds**

1 large **onion**, sliced

2 teaspoons peeled and grated fresh **root ginger**

4 **garlic cloves**, sliced

1 teaspoon **turmeric**

½ teaspoon **chilli powder**

½ teaspoon **ground cinnamon**

1 tablespoon **ground coriander**

1 teaspoon **ground cumin**

3 **tomatoes**, skinned, deseeded and roughly chopped

1 tablespoon **palm sugar** or **soft brown sugar**

200 ml (7 fl oz) **coconut milk**

pinch of **saffron threads**

150 ml (¼ pint) **water**

500 g (1 lb) **monkfish fillet**, cubed

4 tablespoons chopped **coriander leaves**, plus sprigs for garnishing

salt and **pepper**

continued opposite ...

Curried monkfish

Monkfish has a thick meaty texture that makes it ideal for using in curry dishes. Serve this curry with mushroom and olive pilau for a delicious combination.

1 Heat 1 tablespoon of the olive oil in a small frying pan and fry the mustard seeds until they begin to pop, then set aside.

2 Heat the remaining oil in a large, deep frying pan over a moderate heat and fry the onion for 4–5 minutes until soft and browned at the edges. Add the ginger and garlic and fry for a further 2 minutes. Add the spices and cook for 1–2 minutes, stirring constantly.

3 Add the tomatoes, sugar, coconut milk, saffron and fried mustard seeds. Pour in the measured water, season well with salt and pepper and bring the mixture to simmering point. Leave over a low heat for about 15 minutes.

PREP **20**   COOK **50**   SERVES **4**   robust

MUSHROOM AND
OLIVE PILAU:

2 tablespoons **olive oil**

4 **cardamom pods**

2 **cloves**

200 g (7 oz) **button mushrooms**, roughly chopped

65 g (2¼ oz) **pitted black olives**, chopped

300 g (10 oz) **basmati rice**

¼ teaspoon **salt**

500 ml (17 fl oz) boiling **water**

4 Meanwhile, cook the pilau. Heat the olive oil in a large saucepan, add the cardamom, cloves and mushrooms and fry gently until the mushrooms are soft and golden and the spices release an aromatic smell. Add the chopped olives, rice, salt and the measured water and bring to the boil. Reduce the heat, cover the pan and leave to simmer gently for 10–12 minutes until the rice is cooked.

5 Stir the monkfish into the curry sauce and simmer gently for 7–8 minutes or until cooked. Stir in the chopped coriander. Serve the monkfish with the fluffy pilau rice and sprinkled with the coriander sprigs.

750 g (1½ lb) **cod fillet**, skinned

2 tablespoons **plain flour**

4 tablespoons **vegetable oil**

2 **onions**, sliced

2 **garlic cloves**, crushed

1 teaspoon **turmeric**

4 **green chillies**, deseeded and finely chopped

2 tablespoons **lemon juice**

175 ml (6 fl oz) **thick coconut milk** (see page 15)

salt

TO GARNISH:

slices of **red chilli**

snipped **chives**

Fish curry with coconut milk

This simple curry uses spices and coconut milk to enhance the meaty flavour of the cod.

1 Cut the fish into 4 and coat with the flour. Heat the oil in a frying pan. Add the fish and fry quickly on both sides. Lift out with a slotted spoon and set aside.

2 Add the onion and garlic to the pan and fry for about 5 minutes until soft and golden. Add the turmeric, chillies, lemon juice, coconut milk and salt to taste and simmer for 10 minutes or until thickened.

3 Add the fish and any juices, spoon over the sauce and cook gently for 2–3 minutes until tender. Garnish with slices of chilli and snipped chives and serve at once.

PREP
10

COOK
20

SERVES
4

creamy

Thai steamed fish curry

Steaming is used a lot in Thai cuisine and this is a good way to cook fish as it ensures the flesh doesn't break up. All the flavours are concentrated in the covered dish to maximise taste.

1 Mix together the Thai red curry paste, coconut milk, fish sauce and beaten egg. Set aside.

2 Place the fish pieces in a shallow non-metallic dish. Add the coriander, mint and Thai sweet basil and gently mix together. Pour the curry paste mixture over the fish and stir to coat evenly.

3 Scatter the lime rind and chilli slices over the fish. Cover the dish with foil and steam over boiling water for 15 minutes or until the fish is just cooked through. The egg will lightly thicken the sauce. Serve immediately.

3 tablespoons **red curry paste** (see page 16)

200 ml (7 fl oz) **coconut milk**

1 tablespoon **fish sauce**

1 **egg**, beaten

500 g (1 lb) skinless **cod** or **halibut fillets**, cut into 5 cm (2 inch) pieces

1 tablespoon chopped **coriander**

1 tablespoon chopped **mint**

1 tablespoon chopped **Thai sweet basil**

1 tablespoon grated **lime rind**

1 large **green chilli**, deseeded and finely sliced

1 large **red chilli**, deseeded and finely sliced

PREP
10

COOK
15

SERVES
4

healthy

2 tablespoons **oil**

1 teaspoon peeled and finely chopped fresh **root ginger**

1 **green chilli**, deseeded and finely chopped

1 **onion**, chopped

1 **garlic clove**, crushed

1 teaspoon **turmeric**

2 teaspoons **ground coriander**

1 teaspoon grated **lime rind**

2 teaspoons **lime juice**

750 g (1½ lb) **cod fillet**, skinned and cut into bite-sized pieces

150 ml (¼ pint) **coconut milk**

salt and **pepper**

Caribbean fish curry

Fish features heavily in Caribbean cookery and here it is combined with coconut milk and spices to produce a quick, delicious curry that's ready in minutes.

1 Heat the oil in a large frying pan over a moderate heat. Add the ginger and chilli and cook briefly for 10 seconds. Add the onion and garlic and cook for 3 minutes, until the onion is softened but not browned.

2 Stir in the turmeric and coriander and cook gently for 1 minute. Add the lime rind, lime juice, the fish pieces and the coconut milk, and season with salt and pepper to taste. Cook gently for 10 minutes, stirring occasionally, being careful not to break up the fish.

3 When the fish is cooked, lift it out on to a warmed serving plate. Let the sauce simmer for 1 minute. Pour it over the fish and serve immediately.

PREP 10   COOK 15   SERVES 4   quick

Hot and sour fish curry

The hot element of this dish comes from the curry paste, while the sour comes from the tamarind liquid. Use a homemade fish stock to ensure an authentic flavour.

1 Poach the fish in a pan of gently simmering water for 10–15 minutes, until cooked.

2 Lift the fish out of the pan and remove the skin. Put the flesh into a mortar and pound until it is soft and pulpy. Add the curry paste and mix it in well.

3 Heat the stock in a saucepan, add the fish paste and bring to the boil, stirring constantly. Reduce the heat and add the baby sweetcorn, Chinese leaves, sugar and fish sauce and simmer gently for 10 minutes.

4 Stir in the tamarind liquid, simmer for 5 minutes and serve immediately.

150 g (5 oz) firm, boneless, white fish, such as **haddock** or **cod**

1 tablespoon **red curry paste** (see page 16)

900 ml (1½ pints) **fish stock**

4 **baby sweetcorn**, diagonally sliced

100 g (3½ oz) **Chinese leaves**, chopped

2 tablespoons **sugar**

5 tablespoons **fish sauce**

1 quantity **tamarind liquid** (see page 17), made with 1 tablespoon pulp soaked in 150 ml (4 fl oz) boiling water

PREP
4

COOK
30

SERVES
2

quick

4 fresh **tuna steaks**, about 150 g (5 oz) each

juice of 1 **lime**

4 large pieces of **banana leaf**, dipped in boiling water to soften

GREEN CURRY PASTE:

1 tablespoon **cumin seeds**

2 tablespoons **coriander seeds**

3 large **green chillies**, deseeded and chopped

25 g (1 oz) **mint leaves**

5 cm (2 inch) piece of fresh **root ginger**, peeled and grated

4 **garlic cloves**, crushed

25 g (1 oz) **caster sugar**

½ teaspoon **salt**

75 g (3 oz) **desiccated coconut**

50 ml (2 fl oz) **malt vinegar**

TO GARNISH:

lime wedges

fine strips of **lemon rind**

1 **red chilli**, cut into rings

Tuna curry in banana leaves

This is a very fresh-tasting curry. If banana leaves are unavailable, wrap the tuna steaks in a double thickness of buttered greaseproof paper for steaming.

1 Place the tuna steaks in a shallow, non-metallic dish and pour over the lime juice. Cover and set aside to marinate while preparing the curry paste.

2 Place the cumin and coriander seeds in a blender or food processor and process briefly. Add the chillies, mint, ginger and garlic, and work for 1 minute to produce a paste. Add the sugar, salt, coconut and vinegar, and blend again until all the ingredients are thoroughly combined.

3 Lay the pieces of banana leaf (or buttered greaseproof paper) on a flat surface. Remove the tuna from the lime juice and place a steak in the centre of each banana leaf. Spread the green curry paste over the tuna, completely covering the fish. Wrap up the banana leaves to enclose the fish, and secure with cocktail sticks.

4 Steam the fish over a pan of boiling water for 18–20 minutes, or until the fish flakes when tested with the point of a knife.

5 Garnish the steamed fish with lime wedges, lemon rind and chilli rings.

PREP **15**   COOK **20**   SERVES **4**   **fresh**

Coconut fish

This fish curry is light and fresh, with the combination of ginger, coconut and lemon juice resulting in an aromatic dish, packed full of flavour. It is also very quick and simple to prepare.

1 Heat the oil in a large frying pan, add the chillies, garlic and ginger and fry gently for 3 minutes. Add the creamed coconut and, when bubbling, add the pieces of fish and season with salt to taste. Stir well.

2 Cook for 3–4 minutes, stirring constantly and breaking up the fish as it cooks.

3 As soon as all the fish is cooked through, pour in the lemon juice, stir well and serve immediately, garnished with coconut shavings and strips of lemon rind.

2 tablespoons **vegetable oil**

4 **green chillies**, deseeded and chopped

2 **garlic cloves**, finely chopped

2.5 cm (1 inch) piece of fresh **root ginger**, peeled and finely chopped

125 g (4 oz) **creamed coconut**

1 kg (2 lb) thick **haddock fillets**, skinned and cubed

8 tablespoons **lemon juice**

salt

TO GARNISH:

coconut shavings

fine strips of **lemon rind**

PREP
15

COOK
10

SERVES
4

light

3 tablespoons **green curry paste** (see page 15)

400 ml (14 fl oz) can **coconut milk**

1 **lemon grass stalk** (optional)

2 **kaffir lime leaves** (optional)

1 tablespoon **palm sugar** or **soft brown sugar**

1 teaspoon **salt**

300 g (10 oz) **monkfish**, cubed

75 g (3 oz) **green beans**, trimmed

12 raw **tiger prawns**, peeled and deveined

3 tablespoons **fish sauce**

2 tablespoons **lime juice**

TO GARNISH:

sprigs of **coriander**

sliced **green chillies**

Thai monkfish and prawn curry

A firm, meaty fish, monkfish is ideal for curries as its robust texture means it won't break up while cooking. Team it with tiger prawns, which will cook in just a couple of minutes in the sauce.

1 Put the curry paste and coconut milk in a saucepan with the lemon grass and lime leaves, if using, sugar and salt. Bring to the boil, then add the monkfish. Simmer gently for 2 minutes, then add the beans and cook for a further 2 minutes.

2 Remove the pan from the heat and stir in the prawns, fish sauce and lime juice. The prawns will cook in the residual heat, but you will need to push them under the surface of the liquid.

3 Transfer the curry to a warm serving dish and top with coriander sprigs and chilli slices.

PREP **10** COOK **10** SERVES **4** **hearty**

Malaysian fish curry

Swordfish works well in an Asian fish curry, as it doesn't fall apart during cooking. If you use one of the softer-fleshed, flakier white fish instead, reduce the cooking time and keep it in very big chunks.

1 Cut the swordfish steaks into chunky pieces, discarding the skin and any bones. Season with salt and pepper.

2 Roughly chop 2 of the shallots and put them in a food processor with 1 of the garlic cloves, the ginger, turmeric, chilli and 2 tablespoons of the coconut milk. Blend to a smooth paste, scraping the mixture down from the side of the bowl.

3 Scrape the paste into a large saucepan and add the remaining coconut milk, curry leaves and sugar. Bring to the boil, then reduce the heat and simmer gently for 5 minutes. Lower in the fish and cook gently for a further 10 minutes.

4 Finely slice the remaining shallot. Heat the oil in a small frying pan. Add the shallot, the remaining garlic and cumin and fennel seeds and fry gently for 3 minutes. Stir in the coriander leaves, spoon over the curry and serve.

750 g (1½ lb) **swordfish steaks**

3 **shallots**

2 **garlic cloves**, thinly sliced

15 g (½ oz) fresh **root ginger**, peeled and chopped

¼ teaspoon **turmeric**

1 **red chilli**, deseeded and chopped

400 ml (14 fl oz) can **coconut milk**

6 **curry leaves**

2 teaspoons **palm sugar** or **soft brown sugar**

3 tablespoons **vegetable oil**

1 tablespoon **coriander seeds**, crushed

2 teaspoons **cumin seeds**, crushed

2 teaspoons **fennel seeds**, crushed

15 g (½ oz) **coriander leaves**, chopped

salt and **pepper**

PREP
20

COOK
20

SERVES
4

creamy

750 g (1½ lb) **mackerel fillets**

1 teaspoon **salt**

juice of ½ **lemon**

1 large **onion**, finely chopped

4 **garlic cloves**, crushed

1 tablespoon peeled and grated fresh **root ginger**

1 teaspoon **turmeric**

1 teaspoon **dried shrimp paste**

1 tablespoon **sambal oelek** (hot pepper condiment)

1 **lemon grass stalk**, halved lengthways

300 ml (½ pint) **coconut milk**

1 quantity **tamarind liquid** (see page 17) made with 1 tablespoon tamarind pulp soaked in 150 ml (¼ pint) boiling water

3 tablespoons **chopped coriander leaves**

25 g (1 oz) **creamed coconut**, finely grated

TO GARNISH:

a few sprigs of **coriander**

Indonesian fish curry

You should be able to find sambal oelek in Asian grocers or larger supermarkets. It's an important ingredient in Indonesian cookery so worth buying if you plan to cook a lot of curries.

1 Wash the mackerel fillets and pat dry on kitchen paper. Cut each fillet into pieces measuring about 7.5 cm (3 inches) x 5 cm (2 inches). Rub the fillets with ½ teaspoon of the salt and the lemon juice. Set aside.

2 Place the remaining salt, onion, garlic, ginger, turmeric, shrimp paste, sambal oelek, lemon grass and coconut milk in a wide sauté pan. Bring to simmering point, then reduce the heat and cook gently for 15 minutes until the sauce has thickened slightly.

3 Add the tamarind liquid to the sauce. Stir well and cook gently for a further 5 minutes.

4 Add the mackerel and chopped coriander and cook over a low heat for 6–7 minutes until the fish is cooked.

5 Stir in the grated coconut and cook for 3 minutes or until the coconut has dissolved. Serve garnished with coriander sprigs.

PREP **30**

COOK **35**

SERVES **6**

spicy

Fresh crab curry with chillies

You should be able to buy dressed crab at the fish counter of larger supermarkets or at your local fishmonger. Alternatively, you can buy a cooked crab and prepare the meat yourself.

1 Mix the curry powder with the measured water in a saucepan and bring to the boil.

2 Stir in the crab meat. Allow the liquid to return to the boil and add the spring onions, chillies, sugar, wine, salt and pepper. Lower the heat and simmer for 10 minutes.

3 Meanwhile, combine the egg and cream in a small bowl. Mix well, beat in 2 tablespoons of the curry sauce and return the mixture to the saucepan. Stir over a gentle heat for 1 minute, transfer to a serving bowl or even a clean crab shell, if you like, and garnish with dried mango slices, prawn crackers and extra chilli slices.

1 teaspoon **curry powder**

250 ml (8 fl oz) **water**

500 g (1 lb) dressed **crab meat** (see page 15)

4 **spring onions**, chopped

2 **red chillies**, deseeded and finely sliced

1½ teaspoons **sugar**

1 tablespoon **white wine**

½ teaspoon **salt**

¼ teaspoon **pepper**

1 **egg**

1 tablespoon **single cream**

TO SERVE:

dried mango slices

prawn crackers

sliced **red chillies**

PREP
15

COOK
20

SERVES
4

tasty

4 **eggs**, beaten

150 g (5 oz) flaked **crab meat** (see page 15)

2 **shallots**, finely chopped

1 large **red chilli**, deseeded and finely chopped

1 tablespoon chopped **coriander leaves**, plus 2 tablespoons to garnish

1 teaspoon **lemon juice**

1 tablespoon **vegetable oil**

salt and **pepper**

CURRY SAUCE:

3 **shallots**, chopped

2 **red chillies**, deseeded and chopped

3 tablespoons **desiccated coconut**

½ teaspoon **fennel seeds**, lightly crushed

3 tablespoons **vegetable oil**

1 tablespoon **ground coriander**

1 teaspoon **ground cumin**

½ teaspoon **chilli powder**

250 g (8 oz) ripe **tomatoes**, roughly chopped

¼ teaspoon **salt**

1 teaspoon **lemon juice**

300 ml (½ pint) **water**

Ceylon crab omelette curry

Omelette curry is a Sri Lankan speciality and the addition of crab makes it really delicious. Do try to use fresh crab meat in this dish if possible, although canned crab meat may be used instead.

1   To prepare the omelette, place the beaten eggs in a large bowl and add the crab meat, shallots, chilli, coriander and lemon juice. Season the mixture generously with salt and pepper and mix everything together until well combined.

2   Heat the oil in a heavy-based frying pan and pour in the omelette mixture. Cook the omelette over a medium heat for 5 minutes or until it is firm underneath, then place the omelette pan under a preheated grill and cook the omelette for a further 5 minutes or until it is cooked through. Remove the cooked omelette from the pan, roll it up and set it aside while preparing the curry sauce.

PREP **10**

COOK **30**

SERVES **4**

tangy

3 Place the shallots, chillies, coconut and fennel seeds in a blender or food processor and blend briefly to produce a paste. Heat the oil in a large heavy-based saucepan, add the ground coriander, cumin and chilli powder, then fry the mixture over a gentle heat for a few seconds or until fragrant. Add the shallots and chilli paste to the pan and fry gently, stirring occasionally, for about 5 minutes.

4 Stir in the tomatoes, salt, lemon juice and the measured water. Bring the curry sauce to the boil, then reduce the heat and simmer for about 10 minutes. Taste and adjust the seasoning if necessary.

5 Just before serving, cut the rolled up omelette into thick strips and add it to the curry sauce. Heat gently for a further 3–4 minutes, then serve the curry at once, garnished with coriander.

Crab curry

1 tablespoon **vegetable oil**

1½ teaspoons **red curry paste** (see page 16)

6 tablespoons **coconut milk**

1 **lime leaf**, torn

12 **crab claws**

150 ml (¼ pint) **fish stock**

2 tablespoons **sugar**

1 teaspoon **salt**

65 g (2½ oz) can **bamboo shoots**, drained and rinsed

TO GARNISH:

½ large **red chilli**, diagonally sliced

coriander leaves

You will need to thoroughly drain and rinse the bamboo shoots before using. This dish is a great option for a quick and impressive dinner party.

1 Heat the oil in a wok, add the curry paste and stir-fry for 30 seconds, then add all the remaining ingredients. Stir well and simmer for 10 minutes. If the liquid level reduces significantly, add more stock.

2 Turn into a bowl and serve, garnished with the chilli and coriander leaves.

PREP
3

COOK
12

SERVES
4

easy

Goan prawn curry

Prawns soak up plenty of flavour and it's important to use the big tiger prawns to create a more impressive dish.

1 Put the chilli powder, paprika, turmeric, garlic, ginger, ground coriander, cumin, palm sugar and the measured water in a bowl. Mix well and transfer to a large saucepan. Bring this mixture to the boil, cover and simmer gently for 7–8 minutes.

2 Add the coconut milk, salt and tamarind paste and bring to a simmer.

3 Stir in the prawns and cook briskly until they turn pink and are just cooked through. Serve hot, garnished with chopped coriander.

1 teaspoon **chilli powder**

1 tablespoon **paprika**

½ teaspoon **turmeric**

4 **garlic cloves**, crushed

2 teaspoons peeled and grated fresh **root ginger**

2 tablespoons **ground coriander**

1 teaspoon **ground cumin**

2 teaspoons **palm sugar** or **soft brown sugar**

300 ml (½ pint) **water**

400 ml (14 fl oz) can **coconut milk**

2 teaspoons **sea salt**

1 tablespoon **tamarind paste**

625 g (1¼ lb) raw **tiger prawns**, peeled and deveined

TO GARNISH:

chopped **coriander leaves**

PREP
10

COOK
15

SERVES
4

spicy

2 tablespoons **groundnut oil**

1 teaspoon **turmeric**

150 ml (¼ pint) **water**

150 ml (¼ pint) **coconut milk**

2 tablespoons **lime juice**

2 teaspoons **palm sugar** or **soft brown sugar**

16 raw **king prawns**, peeled and deveined

salt and **pepper**

SPICE PASTE:

2 **red chillies**, deseeded and chopped

2 **shallots**, chopped

1 **lemon grass stalk**, chopped

2.5 cm (1 inch) piece of fresh **root ginger**, peeled and chopped

¼ teaspoon **shrimp paste** (optional)

TO GARNISH:

4 **spring onions**, sliced into thin strips

thin slices of **coconut**

1 tablespoon **desiccated coconut**

King prawn and coconut curry

You can prepare the spice paste in advance and set aside until you're ready to cook.

1 Put the spice paste ingredients in a blender or spice mill and blend to a thick paste. Alternatively, pound all the ingredients in a mortar with a pestle.

2 Heat the oil in a wok, add the spice paste and turmeric and then cook over a gentle heat, stirring frequently, for 3 minutes.

3 Add the measured water to the wok, mix well and simmer gently for 3 minutes. Stir in the coconut milk, lime juice and sugar and simmer for a further 3 minutes.

4 Add the prawns to the curry and cook for 4–5 minutes, until they turn pink and are cooked through. Season with the salt and pepper to taste.

5 Transfer the curry to a warm serving dish and serve immediately, garnished with spring onions, coconut slices and desiccated coconut.

PREP **10**

COOK **15**

SERVES **4**

spicy

Prawn patia

This distinctively hot, sweet and sour Parsee dish has a thick, dark sauce made with palm sugar, tamarind and fresh ginger.

1 Put the red and green chillies into a food processor with the cumin, onion seeds and garlic and grind to a rough paste or pound with a pestle and mortar. Heat the oil in a large frying pan, add the spice paste and fry for 1–2 minutes, then add the onions and fry, stirring frequently, for 8–10 minutes until golden.

2 Add the ground coriander, turmeric, cayenne pepper and garam masala and cook for 2 minutes, stirring constantly.

3 Add the curry leaves, tomato purée, tamarind liquid, ginger, coriander and sugar and simmer, uncovered, for 15 minutes or until the sauce is thick.

4 Add the prawns and salt and simmer for 5 minutes. Remove from the heat and leave to stand, covered, for 20 minutes to finish cooking in the residual heat. Serve with basmati rice and a simple curried green vegetable.

PREP **20** COOK **55** SERVES **6** hot

6 large **dried red chillies**, chopped

2 **green chillies**, chopped

1 teaspoon **cumin seeds**

1 teaspoon **black onion seeds**

6 **garlic cloves**, crushed

4 tablespoons **vegetable oil**

4 large **onions**, finely chopped

1 teaspoon **ground coriander**

1 teaspoon **turmeric**

1 teaspoon **cayenne pepper**

1 teaspoon **garam masala**

6 **curry leaves**

2 tablespoons **tomato purée**

300 ml (½ pint) **tamarind liquid** (see page 17)

5 cm (2 inch) piece of fresh **root ginger**, peeled and finely chopped

2 tablespoons chopped **coriander leaves**

2 tablespoons **palm sugar** or **soft brown sugar**

1 kg (2 lb) raw **king** or **tiger prawns**, peeled and deveined

½ teaspoon **salt**

1 teaspoon **chilli powder**

1 teaspoon **paprika**

½ teaspoon **turmeric**

3 **garlic cloves**, crushed

2 teaspoons peeled and finely grated fresh **root ginger**

2 tablespoons **ground coriander**

2 teaspoons **ground cumin**

1 tablespoon **palm sugar** or **soft brown sugar**

400 ml (14 fl oz) **water**

1 **green mango**, stoned and thinly sliced

400 ml (14 fl oz) can half-fat **coconut milk**

1 tablespoon **tamarind paste**

1 kg (2 lb) raw **tiger prawns**, peeled and deveined

salt

Mango and prawn curry

Rich and full-flavoured, this spicy curry from Goa offers the perfect balance of sweet and sharp, spicy and creamy, and smooth and chunky. The green mango, used here as a vegetable, gives the curry a great texture.

1 Put the chilli powder, paprika, turmeric, garlic, ginger, ground coriander, cumin and palm sugar into a large wok with the measured water and stir to mix well. Place over a high heat and bring the mixture to the boil. Reduce the heat and cook covered for 8–10 minutes.

2 Add the mango, coconut milk and tamarind paste and stir to combine. Bring the mixture back to the boil and add the prawns.

3 Stir and cook gently for 8–10 minutes or until all the prawns have turned pink and are cooked through. Season to taste and serve.

PREP **10**   COOK **25**   SERVES **4**   spicy

Prawn curry with onion and garlic

Cumin is one of the most subtle and delicate of all the Indian spices. It blends remarkably well with coriander and other spices such as ginger and turmeric, as in this recipe, and goes particularly well with prawns and fish.

1 Heat the ghee or oil in a large heavy-bottomed saucepan. Add the onion and garlic and fry gently over a low heat for 4–5 minutes, until golden and soft.

2 Mix the spices together in a small bowl, then stir in the vinegar to make a smooth paste.

3 Add the spice paste to the onion and garlic mixture in the pan, then fry gently for a further 3 minutes, stirring constantly with a wooden spoon.

4 Tip in the prawns and turn gently with a wooden spoon until they are well coated with the spices. Stir in the measured water and simmer over a gentle heat for 2–3 minutes. Serve the curry immediately, garnished with coriander leaves.

50 g (2 oz) **ghee**, or 1 tablespoon **vegetable oil**

1 small **onion**, sliced

2 **garlic cloves**, sliced

500 g (1 lb) cooked peeled **prawns**

200 ml (7 fl oz) **water**

SPICE PASTE:

2 teaspoons **ground coriander**

½ teaspoon **ground ginger**

1 teaspoon **turmeric**

½ teaspoon **ground cumin**

½ teaspoon **chilli powder**

2 tablespoons **vinegar**

TO GARNISH:

chopped **coriander leaves**

PREP
15

COOK
15

SERVES
4

tasty

750 ml (1¼ pints) **coconut milk**

2 tablespoons **green curry paste** (see page 15)

2 teaspoons ground **galangal** or **ginger**

750 g (1½ lb) raw **king prawns**, peeled and deveined

2 tablespoons **fish sauce**

TO GARNISH:

1 tablespoon **green chilli**, cut into 2.5 cm (1 inch) strips

4 **basil leaves**, shredded

Spicy prawn curry

Galangal has an unusual flavour that is similar to a citrus taste. It is used extensively in Southeast Asian cuisine.

1 Put the coconut milk in a large jug and chill in the refrigerator for at least 1 hour, or until the thick milk rises to the surface. Scoop 250 ml (8 fl oz) off the top and put it into a wok or heavy saucepan. Reserve the remaining coconut milk for later.

2 Bring the thick coconut milk to the boil and then simmer, uncovered, stirring occasionally, until the coconut oil begins to bubble to the surface and the liquid reduces to a quarter of its original volume. Add the curry paste and galangal and bring to the boil. Cook over a medium-high heat until most of the liquid evaporates.

3 Wash the prawns under cold running water. Pat dry and add to the mixture in the wok. Stir-fry for 3–4 minutes until they are firm and pink.

4 Stir in the remaining coconut milk and the fish sauce and simmer for 6–8 minutes, stirring occasionally. Serve garnished with strips of green chilli and basil leaves.

PREP
10*

COOK
35

SERVES
4–6

simple

* plus at least
1 hour chilling

Steamed seafood curry

In Thailand this dish is usually steamed inside a young coconut. If you can buy one, serve the curry from it as an impressive centrepiece for the dinner table.

1 Mix all the ingredients together thoroughly, except for one of the shredded lime leaves, then place in a heatproof bowl and steam, covered, for 10 minutes. Alternatively, place in the coconut, if using, replace the lid and steam for 30 minutes.

2 Remove the lid from the pan or coconut, sprinkle the lime leaf on the curry, then replace the lid and steam for a further 25 minutes (in the bowl) or 30 minutes (in the coconut). Check that the curry is fully cooked and leave it to steam for longer if required.

8 raw **prawns**, peeled but tails left intact

4 **crab claws**

75 g (3 oz) **crab meat** (see page 15)

3 **lime leaves**, finely shredded

2.5 cm (1 inch) **lemon grass stalk**, finely sliced

1 **egg**, beaten

1 tablespoon **red curry paste** (see page 16)

100 ml (3½ fl oz) **coconut milk**

75 g (3 oz) chopped **Chinese leaves**

25 g (1 oz) chopped **cabbage**

1 teaspoon **palm sugar** or **soft brown sugar**

2 tablespoons **fish sauce**

1 large **red chilli**, diagonally sliced

30 g (1¼ oz) **basil leaves**

1 **coconut**, lid cut out and slice removed from the bottom to create a flat base (optional)

PREP
7

COOK
35

SERVES
4

rich

Prawn vindaloo

2 tablespoons **vegetable oil**

300 ml (½ pint) **water**

1 teaspoon **salt**

1 tablespoon **palm sugar** or **soft brown sugar**

500 g (1 lb) cooked peeled **prawns**

SPICE MIXTURE:

6 **dried red chillies**, deseeded and chopped

150 ml (¼ pint) **malt vinegar**

6 **garlic cloves**, chopped

2.5 cm (1 inch) piece of fresh **root ginger**, peeled and grated

1 teaspoon **mustard seeds**, lightly crushed

20 **black peppercorns**, lightly crushed

1 tablespoon **ground coriander**

1 tablespoon **ground cumin**

1 teaspoon **turmeric**

This is a hot curry that combines a number of spices to complement to heat of the chillies. You can use defrosted, frozen prawns for this dish, if you like.

1 To make the spice mixture, mix together the chillies, vinegar, garlic, ginger, mustard seeds and peppercorns in a bowl, then stir in the remaining ingredients.

2 Heat the vegetable oil in a heavy-based saucepan, stir in the spice mixture and cook over a gentle heat, stirring constantly, for 5 minutes. Add the measured water to the pan, stir well, then cover and simmer the sauce gently for 15 minutes

3 Remove the lid from the pan, increase the heat and cook the sauce over a moderate heat for 5 minutes to reduce it to a thick, coating consistency.

4 Stir the salt, sugar and prawns into the sauce. Cook for 3 minutes, or until the prawns are heated through. Serve immediately.

PREP **10**   COOK **30**   SERVES **4**   fiery

Creamy prawn curry

Quick to prepare, this delicious curry is a good choice if you have unexpected guests. The lime rind and juice add a lovely fresh flavour.

1 Heat the oil in a large saucepan and fry the onion, garlic and ginger for 4–5 minutes. Add the coriander, cumin and turmeric and stir-fry for 1 minute.

2 Pour in the coconut milk and stock and bring to the boil. Reduce the heat and simmer for 2–3 minutes. Stir in the prawns and lime rind and juice, then simmer for 3–4 minutes, or until the prawns are pink and cooked through.

3 Stir in the chopped coriander and season the curry generously with salt and pepper. Serve at once, with basmati or jasmine rice as an accompaniment.

2 tablespoons **vegetable oil**

1 **onion**, halved and finely sliced

2 **garlic cloves**, finely sliced

2.5 cm (1 inch) piece of fresh **root ginger**, peeled and finely chopped

1 tablespoon **ground coriander**

1 tablespoon **ground cumin**

½ teaspoon **turmeric**

200 ml (7 fl oz) **coconut milk**

125 ml (4 fl oz) **vegetable stock**

600 g (1 lb 3 oz) raw **tiger prawns**, peeled and deveined

grated rind and juice of 1 **lime**

4 tablespoons finely chopped **coriander leaves**

salt and **pepper**

TO SERVE:

boiled **basmati** or **jasmine rice**

PREP
10

COOK
15

SERVES
4

creamy

2 tablespoons **groundnut oil**

1 **onion**, finely chopped

3 **garlic cloves**, crushed

2.5 cm (1 inch) piece of fresh **root ginger**, peeled and cut into julienne strips

125 g (4 oz) **tomatoes**, roughly chopped

200 ml (7 fl oz) **coconut milk**

½ teaspoon **salt**

juice of 1 **lime**

2 teaspoons **caster sugar**

20 large raw **prawns**, about 375 g (12 oz) total weight

SPICE MIXTURE:

3 tablespoons **desiccated coconut**, lightly toasted

6 small **dried red chillies**, roughly chopped

10 **black peppercorns**

1 teaspoon **cumin seeds**

1 teaspoon **turmeric**

TO GARNISH:

1 **spring onion**, sliced into julienne strips

Kerala prawn curry

Southern Indian curries are traditionally fairly spicy, as is this Kerala prawn curry. The spiciness comes from the number of dried chillies that are used in the recipe.

1 Place the spice mixture ingredients in an electric spice mill and grind to a fine powder, or grind with a pestle and mortar.

2 Heat the oil in a large, heavy-based saucepan, add the onion, garlic and ginger, and cook, stirring occasionally, for about 3 minutes until softened.

3 Stir in the ground spice mixture and cook, stirring constantly, for a further 2 minutes.

4 Add the tomatoes, coconut milk and salt, and simmer for 6–8 minutes to reduce the sauce and thicken it slightly.

5 Stir in the lime juice and sugar, then add the prawns and simmer the curry gently for about 8 minutes, until the prawns have turned pink. Transfer the curry to a serving dish and scatter over the spring onion. Serve at once.

PREP
15

COOK
25

SERVES
4

spicy

Cochin prawn curry

In this classic dish from the Malabar coast, the addition of tamarind adds tang to a coconut milk-based curry.

1 Rub the prawns with the turmeric and salt. Set aside while preparing the curry.

2 Heat the ghee or vegetable oil in a pan and fry the onion, garlic and ginger over a gentle heat for 3 minutes, until softened.

3 Stir in the coriander, curry powder and chillies, and cook for 2 minutes.

4 Add the tamarind liquid to the pan and stir in the coconut milk. Bring the curry gravy to the boil, stirring constantly, then reduce the heat and simmer for 5 minutes or until it has thickened slightly.

5 Stir in the prawns and cook gently for 5 minutes or until they have turned pink and are cooked through. Taste and adjust the seasoning and serve at once.

20 raw peeled **prawns**, approximate weight 300 g (10 oz)

½ teaspoon **turmeric**

1 teaspoon **salt**

2 tablespoons **ghee** or **vegetable oil**

1 **onion**, finely chopped

3 **garlic cloves**, crushed

1 tablespoon peeled and grated fresh **root ginger**

4 tablespoons chopped **coriander leaves**

1 tablespoon **Indian curry powder**

2 **green chillies**, quartered lengthways and deseeded

1 quantity **tamarind liquid**, made with 1 tablespoon pulp dissolved in 150 ml (¼ pint) boiling water (see page 17)

150 ml (¼ pint) **thick coconut milk** (see page 15)

PREP
15

COOK
20

SERVES
4

tangy

32 raw peeled **prawns**, weighing about 15 g (½ oz) each

4 large **garlic cloves**, cut into 16 thin slices

2 large **red chillies**, each deseeded and cut each into 16 chunks

8 **shallots**, halved lengthways

2.5 cm (1 inch) piece of fresh **root ginger**, cut into 16 thin slices

CURRY SAUCE:

1 large **onion**, chopped

4 **garlic cloves**, chopped

2 tablespoons **vegetable oil**

1 teaspoon **turmeric**

½ teaspoon **chilli powder**

½ teaspoon **ground coriander**

¼ teaspoon **salt**

600 ml (1 pint) **fish stock**

2 tablespoons chopped **coriander leaves**

TO GARNISH:

sprigs of **coriander**

1 **red chilli**, sliced

Burmese prawn kebab curry

This is a really unusual dish with mini kebabs as the centrepiece to the curry. You can prepare the kebabs in advance and keep them covered in the refridgerator until you're ready to cook.

1 Prepare the prawn kebabs. Thread 2 prawns, 1 slice of garlic, 1 chunk of red chilli and ½ a shallot followed by 1 slice of ginger on to 16 cocktail sticks. Set aside while preparing the sauce.

2 Place the onion and garlic in a blender or food processor and blend to a coarse paste. Heat the oil in a saucepan, add the paste and fry, stirring frequently, for 5 minutes until golden.

3 Add the turmeric, chilli powder and ground coriander, stir and fry for a further minute. Stir in the salt and fish stock, bring to the boil, then cover the pan and simmer gently, stirring occasionally, for 20 minutes.

4 Add the prawn kebabs to the curry sauce, cover and cook for a further 7–8 minutes to cook the kebabs. Remove the kebabs and keep them warm.

5 Increase the heat to medium and cook, uncovered, for 6–8 minutes to thicken the sauce. Stir in the chopped coriander. Pour the sauce over the kebabs, garnish with the sprigs of coriander and chilli and serve.

PREP **10**   COOK **45**   SERVES **4**   exotic

Cambodian prawn and marrow curry

Marrow isn't an ingredient you find in many curry recipes but it works well here with prawns and coconut milk. It's important to deseed the marrow so it isn't too watery.

1 Place the spice paste ingredients in a blender or food processor and blend to a coarse paste. Heat the oil in a large flameproof casserole, add the spice paste and fry over a gentle heat, stirring for about 8 minutes or until softened and cooked.

2 Add the coconut milk, stir well and simmer gently for 3–4 minutes. Stir the marrow into the sauce, cover the pan and cook gently for 5 minutes.

3 Add the prawns, fish sauce, lemon juice and sugar to the pan. Stir gently to combine all the ingredients and cook the curry, uncovered, for a further 5 minutes until the prawns have turned pink and are cooked through and the marrow is tender. Taste and adjust the seasoning if necessary. Garnish the curry with coriander sprigs and serve immediately.

3 tablespoons **vegetable oil**

300 ml (½ pint) **coconut milk**

250 g (8 oz) peeled and deseeded young **marrow**, cut into 2.5 cm (1 inch) chunks

20 large raw **prawns**, peeled and deveined

2 tablespoons **fish sauce**

1 tablespoon **lemon juice**

1 teaspoon **caster sugar**

SPICE PASTE:

1 **onion**, chopped

4 **garlic cloves**, chopped

1 **lemon grass stalk**, chopped

1 tablespoon peeled and chopped fresh **root ginger**

2 teaspoons **ground coriander**

1 teaspoon **chilli powder**

½ teaspoon **turmeric**

½ teaspoon **fennel seeds**, lightly crushed

TO GARNISH:

sprigs of **coriander**

PREP
25

COOK
25

SERVES
4

spicy

2 tablespoons **groundnut oil**

1 **shallot**, chopped

2 **garlic cloves**, chopped

2 tablespoons **red curry paste** (see page 16)

1 **red chilli**, deseeded and chopped

3 **kaffir lime leaves**, finely shredded

300 ml (½ pint) **coconut milk**

20 raw **king prawns**, peeled and deveined

125 g (4 oz) **cucumber**, peeled, halved lengthways, deseeded and thickly sliced

1 tablespoon **fish sauce**

1 teaspoon **palm sugar** or **soft brown sugar**

TO GARNISH:

chopped **coriander leaves**

Thai red prawn and cucumber curry

This is so quick and easy to make that it's suitable for a speedy midweek supper. The cucumber adds a clean, cool flavour to the dish.

1 First, heat the oil in a wok, add the shallot and garlic and fry over a gentle heat, stirring for about 3 minutes until softened. Add the red curry paste, chilli and lime leaves and fry for a further 1 minute.

2 Next, add the coconut milk, increase the heat and bring the sauce to the boil, then reduce the heat and simmer the sauce gently, stirring occasionally, for 5 minutes.

3 Add the prawns, cucumber, fish sauce and sugar to the wok. Stir to coat the ingredients evenly in the sauce, then simmer the curry gently for 5 minutes or until the prawns have turned pink and are cooked through and the cucumber is tender. Taste and adjust the seasoning, if necessary. Serve the curry hot, garnished with chopped coriander leaves.

PREP **10**   COOK **15**   SERVES **4**   creamy

Thai yellow prawn curry

This classic Thai dish is often popular in restaurants. The versatile paste can also be used for chicken, meat and fish.

1 Place the spice paste ingredients in a blender or food processor and blend to a thick paste. Heat the oil in a wok or saucepan, add the spice paste and fry over a gentle heat, stirring for 4 minutes, until the paste is fragrant. Stir the measured water into the curry paste, bring to the boil and cook over a fairly high heat for 2 minutes to evaporate some of the water.

2 Stir the coconut milk into the spice paste, then add the prawns. Next, cook the curry over a medium heat, stirring occasionally, for about 6 minutes or until the prawns have turned pink and are cooked through.

3 Stir in the fish sauce and lime juice, and taste and adjust the seasoning, if necessary. Transfer the curry to a warmed serving dish, garnish with the spring onions and chillies and serve immediately.

3 tablespoons **groundnut oil**

125 ml (4 fl oz) **water**

250 ml (8 fl oz) **coconut milk**

20 raw **king prawns**, peeled and deveined

2 teaspoons **fish sauce**

1 teaspoon **lime juice**

SPICE PASTE:

2.5 cm (1 inch) piece of fresh **galangal**, finely chopped

1 **lemon grass stalk**, finely chopped

2 **shallots**, chopped

3 **garlic cloves**, chopped

2 teaspoons **turmeric**

1 teaspoon **ground coriander**

1 teaspoon **ground cumin**

1 teaspoon **shrimp paste**

½ teaspoon **chilli powder**

TO GARNISH:

3 **spring onions**, sliced

2 **red chillies**, shredded

PREP 10 · COOK 15 · SERVES 4 · spicy

5 tablespoons **vegetable oil**

75 g (3 oz) **creamed coconut**

500 ml (17 fl oz) boiling **water**

250 g (8 oz) peeled **pineapple**, cut into chunks

1 teaspoon **salt**

20 large raw **prawns**, peeled but tails left intact

SPICE PASTE:

2 tablespoons **coriander seeds**, lightly crushed

2 tablespoons chopped **coriander leaves**

1 tablespoon **turmeric**

½ teaspoon **shrimp paste**

1 **lemon grass stalk**, chopped

5 **shallots**, chopped

3 **garlic cloves**, chopped

3 **red chillies**, deseeded and chopped

5 small **dried red chillies**, soaked in cold water for 10 minutes, then deseeded and chopped

TO GARNISH:

sprigs of **coriander**

pineapple, cut into wedges

Prawn and pineapple curry

You really need to use a fresh pineapple for this recipe as it's a main ingredient. Remove the 'eyes' with a sharp knife before cutting it into chunks.

1 Place the spice paste ingredients in a blender or food processor and blend to a thick paste. Heat the oil in a wok, add the paste and fry over a gentle heat, stirring constantly, for 5 minutes until softened and fragrant.

2 Dissolve 50 g (2 oz) of the creamed coconut in 450 ml (¾ pint) boiling water to create thin coconut milk and dissolve the remaining coconut in 50 ml (2 fl oz) boiling water to create thick coconut milk.

3 Add half of the thin coconut milk to the paste, stir well and then bring it to simmering point. Cook for about 3 minutes until the sauce has thickened, then stir in the remaining thin coconut milk and cook for 2 minutes more.

4 Add the pineapple and salt to the curry sauce. Cook, stirring, for 2 minutes. Add the prawns and cook for a further 5 minutes until the prawns have turned pink.

5 Stir the thick coconut milk into the curry and simmer very gently for 2 minutes to heat it through. Taste and adjust the seasoning if necessary. Garnish with coriander and pineapple and serve hot.

PREP **25** COOK **20** SERVES **4** fruity

Nonya aubergine and prawn curry

The Nonyas of Malaysia are descended from Chinese traders who intermarried with the indigenous Malays and settled in coastal areas. Their cooking is a distinctive blend of Chinese and Malay influences.

1 Place the curry paste ingredients in a blender or food processor and blend to a thick paste. Heat the oil in a large saucepan, add the curry paste and fry over a gentle heat, stirring constantly, for 5 minutes or until fragrant.

2 Add the coconut milk, stir well and bring to the boil, then reduce the heat and simmer gently for 3 minutes to thicken the sauce slightly.

3 Add the aubergines and the salt, stir gently to mix, then cover the pan and simmer gently, stirring occasionally, for 10 minutes or until the aubergines are tender. Stir the prawns into the curry and cook for a further 5 minutes, until the prawns have turned pink and are cooked through. Taste and adjust the seasoning if necessary and serve the curry hot.

3 tablespoons **groundnut oil**

300 ml (½ pint) **coconut milk**

375 g (12 oz) small **aubergines**, cut into 5 mm (¼ inch) slices

¼ teaspoon **salt**

300 g (10 oz) large raw **prawns**, peeled and deveined

CURRY PASTE:

5 **shallots**, chopped

4 large **garlic cloves**, chopped

3 large **red chillies**, deseeded and chopped

1 teaspoon **shrimp paste**

1 teaspoon **turmeric**

½ teaspoon **salt**

PREP
10

COOK
25

SERVES
4

creamy

1 kg (2 lb) **live mussels**

1 tablespoon **vegetable oil**

1 **onion**, finely chopped

4 **garlic cloves**, crushed

3 **green chillies**, finely chopped

1 teaspoon **turmeric**

100 ml (3½ fl oz) **white wine vinegar**

400 ml (14 fl oz) can **coconut milk**

2 teaspoons **sugar**

4 tablespoons chopped **coriander leaves**

sea salt

TO GARNISH:

freshly grated **coconut**

TO SERVE:

crusty **white bread**

Spiced mussel curry

This is best made with live mussels, available from supermarkets and fishmongers.

1 Rinse the mussels under cold, running water and scrape off any beards. Discard any that are open or that do not close when sharply tapped. Drain and set aside.

2 Heat the oil in a large saucepan and add the onion, garlic, chillies and turmeric and fry for 2–3 minutes. Add the mussels, vinegar, coconut milk, sugar and chopped coriander. Stir well, bring to the boil, cover and cook gently for 5–6 minutes, or until all the mussels have opened. Discard any that remain shut.

3 Transfer the mussels into a serving bowl with a slotted spoon, season to taste and pour over the sauce. Garnish with grated coconut and eat with crusty white bread to mop up the juices.

PREP
10

COOK
12

SERVES
4

spicy

Balti seafood curry

This is quite a hot curry, as it contains both curry powder and chilli powder.

1 Heat the oil in a large, heavy-based frying pan or wok, add the onions, garlic and green pepper and fry until soft but not brown. Add the curry powder, chilli powder and flour and cook gently for about 2–3 minutes.

2 Gradually add the measured water, stirring constantly. Bring the mixture to the boil, lower the heat to a gentle simmer, then add the pieces of white fish and cook for 15 minutes.

3 Add the cooked mussels and prawns and the tomatoes to the pan, season with salt and pepper to taste and simmer for a further 5 minutes.

4 Garnish with strips of chilli and serve immediately.

1–2 tablespoons **vegetable oil**

2 **onions**, finely chopped

2 **garlic cloves**, crushed

1 **green pepper**, cored, deseeded and sliced

2 tablespoons **curry powder**

2 teaspoons **chilli powder**

25 g (1 oz) **plain flour**

600 ml (1 pint) **hot water**

500 g (1 lb) **white fish fillets**, skinned and cubed

125 g (4 oz) cooked shelled **mussels**

125 g (4 oz) cooked peeled **prawns**

4 **tomatoes**, skinned, quartered and deseeded

salt and **pepper**

TO GARNISH:

red chillies, cut into thin strips

PREP
30

COOK
30

SERVES
4–6

hot

2 **lemon grass stalks**, roughly chopped

20 **Thai basil leaves**

1 kg (2 lb) **live mussels**, scrubbed and debearded (see page 150)

2 tablespoons **groundnut oil**

2 tablespoons **red curry paste** (see page 16)

5 cm (2 inch) piece of fresh **galangal**, finely chopped

1 large **green chilli**, thinly sliced

2 **kaffir lime leaves**, finely chopped

200 ml (7 fl oz) **coconut milk**

1 tablespoon **fish sauce**

1 teaspoon **palm sugar** or **soft brown sugar**

175 g (6 oz) peeled **pineapple**, cut into bite-sized pieces

TO GARNISH:

sprigs of **Thai basil** (optional)

Siamese pineapple and mussel curry

This curry can be garnished with Thai basil, which has a strong, slightly liquorice flavour.

1 Pour about 2.5 cm (1 inch) water into a large saucepan. Add the lemon grass and Thai basil and bring the water to the boil. Tip in the mussels, cover and steam for 3–4 minutes, or until they have opened. Drain the mussels, discarding the lemon grass, Thai basil and any mussels that have not opened. Set the mussels on one side while preparing the sauce.

2 Heat the oil in a heavy-based saucepan. Add the curry paste, galangal, chilli and lime leaves and fry over a gentle heat, stirring, for about 4 minutes until fragrant. Stir in the coconut milk, fish sauce and sugar and cook for 1 further minute.

3 Reserve a few mussels in their shells to garnish and remove the remaining mussels from their shells. Add the shelled mussels and pineapple to the curry sauce. Stir gently and cook for 2–3 minutes to heat through. Serve the curry hot, garnished with the reserved mussels and Thai basil, if using.

PREP
30

COOK
15

SERVES
4

fruity

Galle fried squid curry

If liked, the squid tentacles can also be cooked in this curry along with the squid rings – it is purely a matter of taste whether or not they are included.

1 Place the curry sauce ingredients in a heavy-based saucepan, season with salt and bring to the boil. Then reduce the heat and simmer the sauce for about 45 minutes until it is very thick.

2 Heat half the oil in a large frying pan and add half the squid. Cook it over a fairly high heat, stirring constantly, for 1–2 minutes or until the squid has turned white and is just cooked. Using a slotted spoon, transfer the squid to the curry sauce and repeat the process with the remaining oil and squid. (If the tentacles are also to be cooked, they will take about 2 minutes and will be tinged with pink when they are done.)

3 Stir the sugar into the squid curry and simmer the curry gently for 5 minutes to heat through. Taste and adjust the seasoning if necessary and serve at once, garnished with curry leaves, if using.

PREP **20**

COOK **60**

SERVES **4–6**

creamy

3 tablespoons **vegetable oil**

1 kg (2 lb) small **squid**, cleaned and cut into 2.5 cm (1 inch) rings

1 teaspoon **palm sugar** or **soft brown sugar**

CURRY SAUCE:

2 small **onions**, finely chopped

3 **garlic cloves**, crushed

8 **curry leaves**

7 cm (3 inch) piece of **cinnamon stick**, broken in half

1 **lemon grass stalk**, bruised

½ teaspoon **ground ginger**

1 teaspoon **turmeric**

1 teaspoon **chilli powder**

1 tablespoon **Sri Lankan spice mixture** (see page 113)

3 tablespoons **lime juice**

600 ml (1 pint) **coconut milk**

salt

TO GARNISH:

curry leaves (optional)

4 tablespoons **vegetable oil**

1 quantity **tamarind liquid** made with 3 tablespoons pulp soaked in 250 ml (8 fl oz) boiling water (see page 17)

2 **tomatoes**, quartered

2 **baby aubergines**, weighing about 50 g (2 oz) each, quartered

2 large **red chillies**, quartered lengthways and deseeded

1 tablespoon **palm sugar** or **soft brown sugar**

½ teaspoon **salt**

375 g (12 oz) small **squid**, cleaned and left whole

SPICE PASTE:

5 small **dried chillies** soaked in cold water for 10 minutes, then deseeded and chopped

8 **shallots**, chopped

3 **lemon grass stalks**, chopped

2 **red chillies**, deseeded and chopped

2.5 cm (1 inch) piece of fresh **galangal**, chopped

2 teaspoons **dried shrimp paste**

1 teaspoon **turmeric**

5 **candlenuts** or **macadamia nuts** (optional)

Assam squid curry

Ask your fishmonger to clean the squid for you if you don't fancy doing it yourself. They look really impressive in this deliciously hot dish.

1 Place the spice paste ingredients in a blender or food processor and blend to a thick paste. Heat the oil in a large saucepan, add the paste and fry over a gentle heat, stirring constantly, for about 5 minutes until softened.

2 Add the tamarind liquid to the pan with the tomatoes, aubergines and chillies. Bring to the boil, then reduce the heat, cover the pan and simmer gently for 12 minutes.

3 Add the sugar, salt and squid to the pan and stir gently to coat the squid in the sauce. Cook the curry over a gentle heat for a further 5 minutes. Taste and adjust the seasoning if necessary, then serve hot.

PREP **40**   COOK **25**   SERVES **4**   **hot**

Squid sambal

A sambal is often served as a side dish but here it is the main event, with squid soaking up the rich, hot flavours.

1 Place the spice paste ingredients in a blender or food processor and blend to a thick paste. Heat the oil in a large saucepan, add the paste and fry over a moderate heat for 8 minutes, stirring constantly, until the paste is cooked and lightly golden.

2 Add the tamarind liquid to the pan with the sugar, paprika and salt. Cook the sambal sauce over a very gentle heat, stirring occasionally, for about 10 minutes.

3 Add the squid rings and tentacles to the pan. Increase the heat and cook the squid sambal, stirring constantly, for 5–6 minutes or until the squid is cooked and the sauce is thick. Serve with sliced cucumber.

3 tablespoons **groundnut oil**

1 quantity **tamarind liquid** (see page 17), made with 1 tablespoon pulp soaked in 150 ml (¼ pint) boiling water

1½ teaspoons **palm sugar** or **soft brown sugar**

2 teaspoons **paprika**

½ teaspoon **salt**

500 g (1 lb) small **squid** with tentacles, cleaned and cut into 2.5 cm (1 inch) rings

SPICE PASTE:

2 large **onions**, chopped

3 **garlic cloves**, chopped

1 teaspoon **dried shrimp paste**

1½ tablespoons **sambal oelek** (hot pepper condiment, see page 128)

1 tablespoon chopped **lemon grass**

TO SERVE:

sliced **cucumber**

PREP
15

COOK
25

SERVES
4

hot

vegetable

375 g (12 oz) **cauliflower florets**

150 ml (¼ pint) **buttermilk**

1 teaspoon **salt**

3 tablespoons **ghee**

1 large **onion**, thinly sliced

2 **garlic cloves**, crushed

1 tablespoon peeled and grated fresh **root ginger**

1 teaspoon **mustard seeds**

1 teaspoon **black mustard seeds**

1 teaspoon **turmeric**

25 g (1 oz) **desiccated coconut**

150 ml (¼ pint) **water**

2 tablespoons chopped **coriander leaves**

pepper

Cauliflower pachadi

This is a traditional dish from Kerala in southern India, in which cauliflower florets are marinated in buttermilk before being cooked.

1 Place the cauliflower florets in a bowl with the buttermilk, salt and some pepper. Mix well to combine the ingredients and set the bowl aside for 2 hours to allow the cauliflower to marinate in the buttermilk.

2 Heat the ghee in a heavy-based saucepan, add the onion, garlic and ginger, and fry over a gentle heat, stirring occasionally, for about 8 minutes, until softened and lightly golden.

3 Add both types of mustard seeds, the turmeric and coconut to the pan, and cook for a further 3 minutes, stirring constantly.

4 Stir in the cauliflower with its buttermilk marinade and the measured water. Bring the curry to the boil, then reduce the heat, cover the pan and simmer gently for 12 minutes or until the cauliflower is tender.

5 Remove the lid, taste and adjust the seasoning if necessary and stir in the chopped coriander. Increase the heat and cook for a further 3–4 minutes to thicken the sauce. Serve hot as a vegetable accompaniment to other curries.

PREP
10*

COOK
30

SERVES
4

rich

* plus 2 hours marinating

Mushroom and chickpea curry

The mushrooms and chickpeas make this a fairly hearty dish. Serve with aromatic rice, which makes the perfect lightly flavoured accompaniment.

1 First cook the rice. Place the rice in a saucepan with the curry leaves, cardomom, cinnamon and salt. Add the measured water and bring to the boil, then cover the pan and cook over a low heat for 10 minutes. Remove the pan from the heat, but leave the rice undisturbed for a further 10 minutes.

2 Meanwhile, melt the butter in a frying pan and fry the onion, garlic, ginger and mushrooms for 5 minutes.

3 Add the curry powder, ground coriander, cinnamon and potatoes, stir, and then add the chickpeas. Season to taste with salt and pepper and add just enough water to cover. Bring to the boil, cover and simmer gently for 15 minutes.

4 While the curry is cooking, toast and roughly chop the cashew nuts. Stir them into the curry with the yogurt, bananas and chopped coriander, if using. Heat through without boiling and serve with the rice.

PREP
5

COOK
25

SERVES
4

hearty

50 g (2 oz) **butter**

1 **onion**, chopped

2 **garlic cloves**, crushed

2.5 cm (1 inch) piece of fresh **root ginger**, peeled and grated

250 g (8 oz) **button mushrooms**

2 tablespoons **hot curry powder**

1 teaspoon **ground coriander**

1 teaspoon **ground cinnamon**

375 g (12 oz) **potatoes**, diced

400 g (13 oz) can **chickpeas**, drained

50 g (2 oz) **cashew nuts**

125 ml (4 fl oz) **Greek yogurt**

2 unripe **bananas**, cut into chunks

chopped **coriander leaves** (optional)

salt and **pepper**

AROMATIC RICE:

375 g (12 oz) **long-grain rice**

12 **dried curry leaves**

3 **cardamom pods**, crushed

1 **cinnamon stick**, crushed

1 teaspoon **salt**

750 ml (1¼ pints) **water**

2 **onions**, thinly sliced

2 **garlic cloves**, finely chopped

1 tablespoon peeled and grated fresh **root ginger**

4 **green chillies**, 2 finely chopped and 2 slit

1 teaspoon **powdered lemon grass** or finely grated **lemon rind**

1 teaspoon **turmeric**

6 **curry leaves**

600 ml (1 pint) **thin coconut milk** (see page 15)

250 g (8 oz) each **courgettes, potatoes, peppers** and **carrots**, sliced

300 ml (½ pint) **thick coconut milk** (see page 15)

salt

Sri Lankan vegetable curry

This hot mixed vegetable curry typifies Sri Lankan cuisine with the inclusion of turmeric, thick and thin coconut milk and curry leaves.

1 Put the onions, garlic, ginger, chopped chillies, lemon grass or lemon rind, turmeric, curry leaves, thin coconut milk and salt in a saucepan. Bring to simmering point and cook gently, uncovered, for 20 minutes.

2 Add the vegetables, slit chillies and thick coconut milk, and cook for a further 20 minutes or until the vegetables are tender. Transfer to a warmed serving dish and serve.

PREP **15**   COOK **50**   SERVES **4–6**   **hot**

Bombay potatoes

Small new potatoes are the perfect size for this classic medium-hot curry.

1 Heat the oil in a large frying pan or wok and stir-fry the curry purée for 2–3 minutes. Add the curry paste, stir and bring the mixture to simmering point. Add the sliced tomatoes.

2 When the sauce is simmering again, add the potatoes and stir gently until they are heated through. Season with aromatic salt to taste, sprinkle with the chopped mixed herbs and serve immediately.

4 tablespoons **vegetable oil**

⅓ quantity **curry purée** (see page 24)

1 tablespoon **mild curry paste** (see page 17)

2 **tomatoes**, thinly sliced

750 g (1½ lb) cooked **new potatoes**

spicy aromatic salt (see page 14)

1 tablespoon chopped **mixed herbs**, to garnish

PREP **5**

COOK **10**

SERVES **4**

filling

1 tablespoon **sunflower oil**

1 large **onion**, halved and thinly sliced

1 teaspoon peeled and finely grated fresh **root ginger**

2 **garlic cloves**, crushed

2 tablespoons **medium curry powder**

400 g (13 oz) can **chopped tomatoes**

1 teaspoon **honey** or **sugar**

8 large **eggs**, hard-boiled, peeled and halved

4 tablespoons **natural yogurt**, to drizzle over

salt

TO GARNISH:

chopped **coriander leaves**

roasted **cumin seeds**

Tomato egg curry

Hard-boiled eggs cooked in a spiced sauce is a popular dish throughout India. Serve them with simple boiled rice or flatbreads and a vegetable accompaniment or salad for a healthy, nutritious meal.

1 Heat the oil in a large, nonstick frying pan and add the onion. Cook over a medium heat for 10–12 minutes until softened and lightly golden. Add the ginger, garlic and curry powder and stir and cook for 1 minute.

2 Stir in the chopped tomatoes and honey or sugar, bring the mixture to the boil, reduce the heat, cover and cook gently for 10–12 minutes, stirring often. Carefully add the eggs to the mixture and heat through gently until warmed. Drizzle over the yogurt, sprinkle over the coriander and cumin seeds, season and serve immediately.

PREP
5

COOK
35

SERVES
4

mellow

Chickpea and potato curry

If you fancy something spicy, healthy and fast, then this is perfect! It is delicious simply with basmati rice, nann or plenty of grainy bread, plus your favourite type of chutney and a salad.

1 Heat the oil in a large saucepan. Add the chopped onion, turmeric, curry paste and potato cubes and fry gently for 5 minutes.

2 Add the chickpeas, tomatoes, sugar and a little salt and pepper. Bring to the boil, then turn down the heat and cook, uncovered, for about 20 minutes, stirring frequently and breaking up the tomatoes.

3 Stir in the chopped coriander and add more salt and pepper if it needs it, then serve.

2 tablespoons **vegetable oil**

1 large **onion**, chopped

1 teaspoon **turmeric**

2 teaspoons **medium curry paste**

1 large **potato**, cut into cubes

400 g (13 oz) can **chickpeas**, drained and rinsed

2 x 400 g (13 oz) cans **plum tomatoes**

2 teaspoons **sugar**

small handful of **coriander leaves**, chopped

salt and **pepper**

PREP
10

COOK
25

SERVES
2

spicy

Cauliflower curry

125 g (4 oz) **ghee** or
2 tablespoons **vegetable oil**

pinch of **asafoetida powder**
(see page 11)

750 g (1½ lb) **cauliflower**,
cut into florets

300 ml (½ pint) **natural
yogurt**

2 large **onions**, finely
chopped

2 **garlic cloves**, crushed

4 **bay leaves**

6 **cloves**

6 **black peppercorns**

1 **black cardamom**

2 **green cardamoms**

2 x 2.5 cm (1 inch) pieces of
cinnamon stick

1 teaspoon **coriander seeds**

1 teaspoon **white cumin
seeds**

1 teaspoon **red chilli
powder**

300 ml (½ pint) hot **water**

salt

Cauliflower is a popular ingredient in Indian vegetarian food as it holds its shape and absorbs plenty of flavour. Don't cut the florets too small or they will overcook.

1 Heat 25 g (1 oz) of the ghee or ½ teaspoon of the vegetable oil in a large saucepan with the asafoetida. Add the cauliflower and cook over a medium heat for 5 minutes. Using a slotted spoon, transfer the cauliflower to a bowl and pour the yogurt over the top.

2 Add the remaining ghee or vegetable oil to the pan and when it is hot, add the onions, garlic, salt to taste, bay leaves and all the spices except the chilli powder. Fry until the onions are golden and soft, then stir in the chilli powder.

3 Return the cauliflower and yogurt to the pan and stir gently to combine all the ingredients. Cook gently over a low heat for 10 minutes.

4 Pour in the measured water and simmer, stirring the curry occasionally, for 25 minutes or until the cauliflower is tender. Serve this curry hot.

PREP **15**

COOK **45**

SERVES **4–6**

spicy

Creamy mixed vegetable curry

The aromatic flavour of cardamom adds an unusual twist to this chunky vegetable curry. You can substitute other vegetables depending on your personal taste and what is in season at the time.

1 Heat the oil in a heavy-based saucepan, add the onion and fry over a gentle heat, stirring occasionally for about 4 minutes or until softened but not coloured. Stir in the cardamom pods, coriander, cumin, chilli powder and turmeric and fry for a further 1 minute.

2 Add the carrots, aubergine, the stock and a good pinch of salt. Stir well, bring to the boil, then reduce the heat and simmer, covered, for 10 minutes, stirring occasionally.

3 Stir in the courgettes, green beans and the yogurt. Cook the curry, uncovered, for 15 minutes, stirring occasionally.

4 Stir in the chopped coriander and cashew nuts. Heat through for 1 minute, then taste and adjust the seasoning if necessary. Transfer the curry to a warm serving dish. Drizzle over the yogurt, garnish with sprigs of coriander and serve hot.

3 tablespoons **vegetable oil**

1 **onion**, finely chopped

6 **cardamom pods**, bruised

2 teaspoons **coriander seeds**, lightly crushed

2 teaspoons **cumin seeds**, lightly crushed

1½ teaspoons **chilli powder**

1 teaspoon **turmeric**

175 g (6 oz) **carrots**, sliced

175 g (6 oz) **aubergine**, roughly chopped

300 ml (½ pint) **vegetable stock**

175 g (6 oz) **courgettes**, sliced

175 g (6 oz) **green beans**, topped and tailed and cut into 2.5 cm (1 inch) lengths

150 ml (¼ pint) **natural yogurt**

2 tablespoons chopped **coriander leaves**

50 g (2 oz) toasted **cashew nuts**, roughly chopped

salt

TO GARNISH:

1 tablespoon **natural yogurt**

sprigs of **coriander**

PREP
10

COOK
35

SERVES
4–6

creamy

500 g (1 lb) waxy **potatoes**

1¼ tablespoons **chilli powder**

3 tablespoons **ghee**

2 large **onions**, sliced thinly

6 **curry leaves**

salt

Tamil dry potato curry

This is a very simple dish relying on the intense flavours of spices being absorbed by the potatoes. Serve with dhal (see page 172).

1 Scrub the potatoes and cook them in a pan of salted boiling water for 25 minutes or until they are cooked. Drain and refresh them in cold water. When they are cool enough to handle, peel and cut them into 2.5 cm (1 inch) chunks. Place the potato chunks in a bowl, add the chilli powder and season generously with salt. Toss to coat the potatoes evenly.

2 Heat the ghee in a large, heavy-based frying pan, add the onions and fry, stirring occasionally, for 5 minutes or until softened and lightly golden.

3 Stir in the chilli-coated potatoes and the curry leaves and fry over a very low heat, stirring, for 10 minutes or until the potatoes and onions are golden and the flavours are well combined. Taste the curry and adjust the seasoning if necessary then serve immediately.

PREP **5**

COOK **45**

SERVES **4–6**

hot

Mushroom curry

Mushrooms act like sponges so will absorb plenty of flavours in this quick and easy curry. The coconut milk adds a creamy finish to the dish.

1 Heat the ghee or oil in a heavy-based frying pan. Add the garlic, ginger and spring onions and fry over a gentle heat, stirring occasionally, for 2 minutes, or until softened.

2 Stir in the curry powder and mustard seeds and cook for a further 1 minute. Add the prepared mushrooms and the salt. Stir well to mix, then cook, covered, for a further 5 minutes, stirring occasionally.

3 Add the garam masala and coconut milk and cook, uncovered, for a further 4–5 minutes, until the sauce has thickened slightly.

4 Stir in the lemon juice. Adjust the seasoning, if necessary, then serve the curry immediately, garnished with coriander sprigs.

2 tablespoons **ghee** or **vegetable oil**

3 **garlic cloves**, crushed

1 teaspoon peeled and grated fresh **root ginger**

6 **spring onions**, sliced

1 tablespoon **curry powder**

½ teaspoon **mustard seeds**

300 g (10 oz) **button mushrooms**, halved

300 g (10 oz) **flat mushrooms**, thickly sliced

1 teaspoon **salt**

1 teaspoon **garam masala**

150 ml (¼ pint) **thick coconut milk** (see page 15)

2 tablespoons **lemon juice**

TO GARNISH:

sprigs of **coriander**

PREP 15

COOK 15

SERVES 4

creamy

2 tablespoons **vegetable oil**

1 **onion**, thinly sliced

3 **garlic cloves**, crushed

2 **red chillies**, deseeded and chopped

½ teaspoon **ground cumin**

½ teaspoon **ground coriander**

1 teaspoon **curry powder**

1 teaspoon **dried shrimp paste**

1 **lemon grass stalk**, finely chopped

2 **tomatoes**, skinned, deseeded and chopped

300 ml (½ pint) **chicken** or **vegetable stock**

300 ml (½ pint) **coconut milk**

125 g (4 oz) **pumpkin**, peeled, deseeded and diced

150 g (5 oz) **white cabbage**, shredded coarsely

150 g (5 oz) **French beans**, topped and tailed, sliced thinly

150 g (5 oz) small **cauliflower florets**

200 g (7 oz) canned **bamboo shoots**, drained

2 tablespoons **roasted peanuts**, roughly chopped

2 teaspoons **lemon juice**

salt

Vegetable and coconut curry

The coconut milk and pumpkin give this dish a sweet flavour which is tempered nicely by the heat of the chillies. Warm naan bread would make an ideal accompaniment.

1 Heat the oil in a saucepan, add the onion, garlic and chillies, and fry over a moderate heat, stirring occasionally for 7 minutes, until softened and lightly coloured.

2 Add the ground cumin, coriander, curry powder, shrimp paste and lemon grass, and fry for a further 2 minutes. Stir in the tomatoes, stock and coconut milk. Bring the sauce to simmering point and add the pumpkin. Cook for 3 minutes, then add the cabbage and cook for a further 2 minutes. Add the beans, cauliflower and bamboo shoots to the pan, cover and cook over a gentle heat for 10–12 minutes or until all the vegetables are tender.

3 Stir the peanuts and lemon juice into the curry and season to taste with salt. Serve the curry hot.

PREP
30

COOK
30

SERVES
4–6

sweet

Aubergine and peanut curry

It's important to add salt to the aubergine as they contain a lot of liquid and the salt helps to draw this out.

1 Rub the salt all over the cubed aubergine and place it in a steamer above a pan of boiling water. Steam the aubergine for about 5 minutes, until it is just tender. Drain and set aside.

2 Heat the oil in a wok, add the shallots and garlic, and fry over a gentle heat, stirring frequently, for 5 minutes, or until softened. Add the shrimp paste and galangal powder, and fry for a further 3 minutes.

3 Add the coconut milk, tamarind, soy sauce, sambal oelek and sugar. Stir well and simmer gently for 3 minutes. Stir the steamed aubergine into the sauce and cook gently for a further 5 minutes. Add the ground peanuts to the curry and cook gently for 2 minutes.

4 Serve the curry immediately with plain boiled rice or nasi guriah.

½ teaspoon **salt**

750 g (1½ lb) **aubergines**, cut into 2.5 cm (1 inch) cubes

3 tablespoons **groundnut oil**

4 **shallots**, chopped

2 **garlic cloves**, crushed

1 teaspoon **dried shrimp paste**

½ teaspoon **galangal powder**

250 ml (8 fl oz) **coconut milk**

1 teaspoon **tamarind paste**

1 tablespoon **dark soy sauce**

1 tablespoon **sambal oelek** (hot pepper condiment)

1 tablespoon **palm sugar** or **soft brown sugar**

125 g (4 oz) **roasted peanuts**, coarsely ground

TO SERVE:

boiled **rice** or **Nasi Guriah** (see page 220)

PREP
10

COOK
25

SERVES
6

hearty

600 ml (1 pint) **thin coconut milk** (see page 15)

3 **shallots**, thinly sliced

1 **lemon grass stalk**, halved lengthways

5 **curry leaves**

2 **garlic cloves**, crushed

2 large **red chillies**, halved lengthways, deseeded and thinly sliced

1 tablespoon peeled and grated fresh **root ginger**

1 teaspoon **black mustard seeds**

¼ teaspoon **turmeric**

½ teaspoon **chilli powder**

¼ teaspoon **ground cinnamon**

1 teaspoon **salt**

250 g (8 oz) raw **cashew nuts**, soaked overnight in cold water

25 g (1 oz) **creamed coconut**, finely chopped

Cashew nut curry

In Sri Lanka, this curry is traditionally made from freshly picked cashew nuts. Raw cashews, soaked overnight, make a good substitute for the very fresh nuts.

1 Place all the ingredients except the cashew nuts and the creamed coconut in a heavy-based saucepan. Stir everything together to combine, bring the mixture to the boil, then reduce the heat and simmer gently, uncovered, for 15 minutes or until the sauce has thickened slightly.

2 Drain the cashew nuts and add them to the pan. Cook over a gentle heat, stirring occasionally, for 20 minutes, or until the nuts are tender.

3 Add the chopped creamed coconut to the pan, stir well to allow it to dissolve and simmer the curry gently for a further 5 minutes, without letting it boil. Taste and adjust the seasoning if necessary. Serve immediately.

PREP
10*

COOK
45

SERVES
4–6

spicy

* plus overnight soaking

Spinach paneer

Paneer is Indian curd cheese and it is available from good Indian grocers and also supermarkets.

1 Cut the paneer into 2.5 cm (1 inch) cubes and set it aside. Steam the spinach for 3–4 minutes until it has wilted, leave it to cool and then place it in a food processor and blend briefly to purée it. Set it aside.

2 Heat the ghee in a heavy-based saucepan, add the paneer cubes and fry them, turning them occasionally, for 10 minutes or until they are golden all over. Remove them from the pan and set aside.

3 Add the onion, garlic, chilli and ginger to the hot ghee and fry gently over a low heat, stirring constantly, for 5 minutes, until softened. Stir in the turmeric, coriander, chilli powder and cumin, and fry for a further minute.

4 Add the puréed spinach and salt, stir well to combine, cover the pan and simmer gently for 5 minutes.

5 Stir in the fried paneer and cook, covered, for a further 5 minutes. Taste and adjust the seasoning if necessary, and serve immediately.

250 g (8 oz) **paneer**

375 g (12 oz) **young leaf spinach**, washed and dried

2 tablespoons **ghee**

1 large **onion**, chopped

2 **garlic cloves**, crushed

1 large **green chilli**, deseeded and sliced

1 tablespoon peeled and grated fresh **root ginger**

1 teaspoon **turmeric**

1 teaspoon **ground coriander**

1 teaspoon **chilli powder**

½ teaspoon **ground cumin**

½ teaspoon **salt**

PREP
15

COOK
30

SERVES
4

fresh

3 tablespoons **mustard oil** or **vegetable oil**

1 large **onion**, sliced

2 **garlic cloves**, crushed

2.5 cm (1 inch) piece of fresh **root ginger**, peeled and finely chopped

1 teaspoon **turmeric**

2 **bay leaves**

2 small **dried red chillies**

250 g (8 oz) **split red lentils**, rinsed

500 ml (17 fl oz) **water**

2 tablespoons **desiccated coconut**

1 teaspoon **chilli powder**

½ teaspoon **cumin seeds**

¼ teaspoon **fennel seeds**

¼ teaspoon **black onion seeds**

1 teaspoon **sugar**

salt and **pepper**

TO GARNISH:

toasted **desiccated coconut**

Masoor dhal

If possible, use mustard oil, which is available from Indian supermarkets, instead of vegetable oil in this recipe to produce a sweeter, more fragrant dish.

1 Heat half the vegetable oil in a heavy-based saucepan, add the onion, garlic and ginger and fry over a gentle heat, stirring frequently, for about 5 minutes or until softened but not coloured. Add the turmeric, bay leaves and chillies and fry for 1 minute.

2 Add the drained lentils and stir to coat them evenly in the spices. Season generously and add the measured water. Bring to the boil, then reduce the heat, cover the pan and simmer gently, stirring occasionally, for 15–20 minutes or until the lentils are cooked.

3 While the dhal is cooking, heat the remaining oil in a small frying pan, add the coconut, chilli powder, cumin, fennel and black onion seeds and fry, stirring, for 2 minutes or until fragrant.

4 Stir the cooked spices into the dhal, with the sugar. Cook, stirring frequently, for a further 3 minutes. Taste and adjust the seasoning if necessary and serve hot, garnished with the toasted desiccated coconut.

PREP **10**

COOK **30**

SERVES **4**

sweet

Okra masala

Okra, also known as 'lady's finger', is a popular ingredient in Indian cuisine, especially from the south of the country. Here, it is combined with a number of spices to create a fragrant dish.

1 Heat the oil in a heavy-based saucepan, add the cumin, fennel, mustard and sesame seeds and fry over a gentle heat, stirring, for 1 minute. Stir in the onion and garlic and then fry, stirring occasionally, for a further 3 minutes.

2 Add 3 tablespoons of water, the sugar, tomato purée and curry paste, mix well and cook over a gentle heat for 1 minute.

3 Stir in the okra and season with salt. Add the measured water to the pan and stir well. Bring the curry to the boil, then reduce the heat and simmer the curry gently for 10 minutes, stirring occasionally, until the okra are tender. Taste and adjust the seasoning if necessary. Serve hot, immediately.

3 tablespoons **groundnut oil**

1 teaspoon **cumin seeds**

½ teaspoon **fennel seeds**

½ teaspoon **mustard seeds**

1 teaspoon **sesame seeds**

1 **onion**, finely chopped

2 **garlic cloves**, crushed

1 tablespoon **palm sugar** or **soft brown sugar**

1 tablespoon **tomato purée**

2 tablespoons **Madras curry paste**

500 g (1 lb) small **okra**, stalks trimmed

200 ml (7 fl oz) **water**

salt

PREP
5

COOK
20

SERVES
6

light

250 g (8 oz) **long-grain rice**

1 tablespoon **olive oil**

2 **carrots**, chopped

1 large **potato**, chopped

2.5 cm (1 inch) piece of fresh **root ginger**, peeled and grated

2 **garlic cloves**, crushed

150 g (5 oz) **cauliflower florets**

100 g (3½ oz) **green beans**, cut in half

1 tablespoon **hot curry paste**

1 teaspoon **turmeric**

½ teaspoon **ground cinnamon**

150 ml (¼ pint) **natural yogurt**

25 g (1 oz) **raisins**

TO GARNISH:

50 g (2 oz) **cashew nuts**, toasted

2 tablespoons chopped **coriander leaves**

Vegetable biryani

This dish is fresh and fragrant. If you can't cope without meat in your diet, then add some cooked chicken at the same time as you add the yogurt.

1 Cook the rice in water according to the instructions on the packet and drain.

2 Meanwhile, heat the oil in a saucepan, add the carrots, potato, ginger and garlic and fry for 10 minutes until soft.

3 Stir in the cauliflower, beans, curry paste, turmeric and cinnamon and cook for 1 minute.

4 Stir in the yogurt and raisins. Pile the rice on top of the vegetables, cover and cook over a low heat for 10 minutes, checking it isn't sticking to the pan.

5 Serve the biryani sprinkled with the cashew nuts and chopped coriander leaves.

PREP
10

COOK
20

SERVES
2

fresh

Pumpkin, chickpea and banana curry

This combination of flavours may sound rather unusual, but the different tastes work together really well. Try it and you'll be converted!

1 Heat 2 tablespoons of the oil in a heavy-based saucepan, add the onion, garlic, ginger and ground spices and fry over a medium heat for 5–6 minutes until the onion is lightly browned.

2 Put the pumpkin in a bowl, add the curry paste and toss well so the pumpkin is coated.

3 Add the tomatoes, chillies and vegetable stock to the onion mixture, bring to the boil and simmer gently for 15 minutes.

4 Meanwhile, heat the rest of the oil in a frying pan, add the pumpkin and fry for 5 minutes until golden.

5 Add the diced pumpkin to the tomato sauce with the chickpeas, cover and cook for 15 minutes until the pumpkin is tender.

6 Mix the banana into the curry and cook for 5 more minutes, then stir in the coriander. Serve immediately with rice or nann bread.

3 tablespoons **vegetable oil**

1 small **onion**, sliced

2 **garlic cloves**, chopped

2 teaspoons peeled and grated fresh **root ginger**

1 teaspoon **ground coriander**

½ teaspoon **ground cumin**

½ teaspoon **turmeric**

¼ teaspoon **ground cinnamon**

500 g (1 lb) **pumpkin**, peeled, deseeded and diced

2 tablespoons **hot curry paste**

2 **tomatoes**, chopped

2 **dried red chillies**

300 ml (½ pint) **vegetable stock**

400 g (13 oz) can **chickpeas**, drained and rinsed

1 large under-ripe **banana**, thickly sliced

1 tablespoon chopped **coriander leaves**

TO SERVE:

rice or **nann bread**

PREP
25

COOK
50

SERVES
4

sweet

500 g (1 lb) **sweet potatoes**, peeled and cut into large chunks

3 tablespoons **vegetable oil**

1 **red onion**, chopped

2 **garlic cloves**, crushed

1 teaspoon **turmeric**

1 large **red chilli**, deseeded and chopped

400 ml (14 fl oz) **coconut milk**

250 g (8 oz) **baby spinach**, washed

salt

TO SERVE:

nann bread or **chapattis**

Sweet potato and spinach curry

Everyone loves a good curry, and friends and family are bound to be impressed when you serve up this extremely tasty dish.

1 Cook the sweet potato in a large saucepan of boiling water for 8–10 minutes, then drain and put to one side.

2 Heat the oil in a saucepan, add the onion, garlic and turmeric and fry over a gentle heat, stirring often, for 3 minutes. Stir in the chilli and fry for another 2 minutes.

3 Add the coconut milk, stir well, then simmer for 3–4 minutes until the coconut milk has thickened slightly. Stir in the cooked sweet potatoes and a dash of salt, then cook the curry for 4 minutes.

4 Stir in the baby spinach, cover the pan and simmer gently for 2–3 minutes, or until the spinach has wilted and the curry has heated through. Serve immediately with nann bread or chapattis.

PREP 15   COOK 25   SERVES 4   easy

Mixed bean curry

Supremely good for you, this three-bean curry is packed with protein and tasty spices, and it tastes delicious.

1 Heat the butter in a saucepan and fry the onions for 10 minutes until golden brown. Add the garlic and fry for a few seconds only, then add the coriander, garam masala and chilli powder and fry for a few seconds. Stir in the tomatoes and sugar with a dash of salt and pepper, then turn down the heat and cook for 10 minutes.

2 Add all the beans, stir thoroughly, then cover and cook gently until heated through. Delicious served with rice and poppadums.

125 g (4 oz) **butter**

2 **onions**, finely chopped

3 **garlic cloves**, crushed

1 tablespoon **ground coriander**

1 teaspoon **garam masala**

1 teaspoon **chilli powder**

400 g (13 oz) can **chopped tomatoes**

1 teaspoon **sugar**

425 g (14 oz) can **butter beans**, drained and rinsed

425 g (14 oz) can **red kidney beans**, drained and rinsed

425 g (14 oz) can **cannellini beans**, drained and rinsed

salt and **pepper**

TO SERVE:

rice or **poppadums**

PREP
25

COOK
30

SERVES
4

filling

300 ml (½ pint) **coconut milk**, plus extra for drizzling

40 g (1½ oz) **green curry paste** (see page 15)

300 ml (½ pint) **vegetable stock**

4 small round **aubergines**, each cut into 8 pieces

40 g (1½ oz) **palm sugar** or **soft brown sugar**

1 teaspoon **salt**

4 teaspoons **soy sauce**

25 g (1 oz) fresh **root ginger**, peeled and finely chopped

425 g (14 oz) can **straw mushrooms**, drained

50 g (2 oz) **green pepper**, thinly sliced

Green curry with straw mushrooms

Green curry is best served with rice or noodles as they will soak up the delightfully creamy sauce.

1 Heat the coconut milk in a saucepan with the curry paste, stirring well to combine the two. Add the stock and then the aubergines, sugar, salt, soy sauce, ginger and mushrooms.

2 Bring to the boil and cook, stirring, for 2 minutes. Add the green pepper, turn down the heat and cook for 1 minutes. Serve in a bowl, drizzled with a little extra coconut milk.

PREP **7**

COOK **10**

SERVES **4**

quick

Mushroom and pea curry

If fresh peas are in season then you can substitute these for the frozen. To clean the mushrooms, rub them over with a piece of kitchen towel.

1 Heat the oil in a large saucepan, add the onion and fry gently for 2–3 minutes until it begins to soften. Add the cumin and mustard seeds and fry, stirring, for another 2 minutes.

2 Add the tomatoes, chilli, mushrooms and peas. Stir and cook for 2 minutes.

3 Add the chilli powder and turmeric, mix well, then cook, uncovered, for 5–7 minutes.

4 Add the red pepper, garlic and coriander and fry for 5 minutes until the mixture is quite dry. Serve immediately.

2 tablespoons **vegetable oil**

50 g (2 oz) **onion**, finely sliced

¼ teaspoon **cumin seeds**, crushed

¼ teaspoon **mustard seeds**

125 g (4 oz) **tomatoes**, chopped

1 **green chilli**, deseeded and finely chopped

425 g (14 oz) **button mushrooms**, halved (quartered if large)

150 g (5 oz) frozen **peas**

½ teaspoon **chilli powder**

¼ teaspoon **turmeric**

1 **red pepper**, cored, deseeded and chopped

4 **garlic cloves**, crushed

2 tablespoons **coriander leaves**

PREP
10

COOK
20

SERVES
4

spicy

500 ml (17 fl oz) **natural yogurt**

2 tablespoons **gram flour** (besan)

2 tablespoons **vegetable oil**

½ teaspoon **ground cumin**

½ teaspoon **ground coriander**

2 **garlic cloves**, crushed

2 **green chillies**, finely chopped

2 **red chillies**, finely chopped

1 teaspoon **turmeric**

1 tablespoon chopped **coriander leaves**

6 **curry leaves**

salt

TO GARNISH:

curry leaves

1 **red chilli**, deseeded and cut into rings

Yogurt curry

This simple flavoured yogurt dish would work well served alongside a dry curry.

1 Mix the yogurt and gram flour together.

2 Heat the oil in a pan, add the cumin, ground coriander, garlic and chillies and fry for 1 minute. Stir in the turmeric, then immediately pour in the yogurt mixture. Add salt to taste and simmer, uncovered, for 10 minutes, stirring occasionally.

3 Add the chopped fresh coriander and the curry leaves and continue cooking for a further 5 minutes.

4 Transfer to a warmed serving dish and serve, garnished with curry leaves and chilli rings. Remove the curry leaves before eating.

PREP **5**

COOK **25**

SERVES **4**

creamy

Chickpea chole

This chickpea dish is a hearty and deliciously fragrant vegetarian curry.

1 Heat the oil in a heavy-based saucepan, add the onion, garlic and ginger and fry over a gentle heat, stirring frequently, for about 5 minutes or until softened but not coloured.

2 Stir in the ground coriander, cumin, chilli powder and turmeric and fry for 2 minutes. Next, add the chickpeas, tomatoes, sugar and some salt to taste, and stir to combine the ingredients. Cover the pan and simmer the curry gently, stirring occasionally, for 10 minutes.

3 Stir in 1 tablespoon of the lime juice and the torn coriander leaves and heat through for a further 2 minutes. Taste the curry and add the remaining lime juice and more salt if necessary. Serve the chole hot, garnished with the coriander sprigs and slices of red onion.

3 tablespoons **vegetable oil**

1 **onion**, chopped

2 **garlic cloves**, crushed

2.5 cm (1 inch) piece of fresh **root ginger**, peeled and grated

1 tablespoon **ground coriander**

4 teaspoons **ground cumin**

2 teaspoons **chilli powder**

1 teaspoon **turmeric**

2 x 400 g (13 oz) cans **chickpeas**, drained and rinsed

400 g (13 oz) can **chopped tomatoes**

1½ teaspoons **palm sugar** or **soft brown sugar**

1–2 tablespoons **lime juice** (depending on taste)

4 tablespoons torn **coriander leaves**

salt

TO GARNISH:

3 sprigs of **coriander**

½ **red onion**, sliced

PREP **10**

COOK **20**

SERVES **4–6**

hearty

25 g (1 oz) **butter**

1 tablespoon **vegetable oil**

2 large **onions**, finely chopped

50 g (2 oz) fresh **root ginger**, peeled and grated

2 **garlic cloves**, crushed

2 **bay leaves**

1 **cinnamon stick**, broken in half

2 teaspoons **fennel seeds**

3 **green cardamoms**

1 teaspoon **turmeric**

1 kg (2 lb) small **new potatoes**

600 ml (1 pint) **water**

300 ml (½ pint) **natural yogurt**

chilli powder, to taste

salt and **pepper**

TO GARNISH:

chopped **coriander leaves**

4 **kaffir lime leaves**

New potato curry

Serve this curry as a main course, accompanied either by a dish of peeled prawns, sprinkled with grated lemon rind and chilli powder, or quartered hard-boiled eggs sprinkled with paprika, chopped thyme and salt and pepper.

1 Heat the butter and oil in a wok. Add the onions, ginger, garlic, bay leaves, cinnamon, fennel seeds, cardamoms and turmeric. Stir-fry for a few minutes until the onion is softened, but not browned.

2 Stir in the potatoes, pour in the measured water and add salt and pepper to taste. Bring to the boil and cover the wok. Simmer for 10 minutes, then uncover and cook fairly rapidly for a further 10 minutes, or until most of the water has evaporated.

3 Pour the yogurt over the potatoes and heat gently to avoid curdling the sauce. Sprinkle with chilli powder to taste before garnishing the curry with chopped coriander and kaffir lime leaves.

PREP **10**

COOK **25**

SERVES **4**

hearty

Pineapple red curry

Fresh pineapple is packed full of flavour and the juice will combine with the other ingredients to produce an unusual, spiced curry.

1 Mix the coconut milk and curry paste together in a saucepan over a low heat.

2 Add the rest of the ingredients and bring slowly to the boil, stirring occasionally. Lower the heat and simmer for 10 minutes. Serve hot.

100 ml (3½ fl oz) **coconut milk**

1 tablespoon **red curry paste** (see page 16)

500 g (1 lb) **pineapple**, chopped

450 ml (¾ pint) **water**

25 g (1 oz) **palm sugar** or **soft brown sugar**

1½ teaspoons **salt**

1 tablespoon **lime juice**

1 tablespoon **soy sauce**

PREP **10**

COOK **15**

SERVES **4**

fruity

600 ml (1 pint) **water**

1 tablespoon **red curry paste** (see page 16)

20 **lychees**, stoned, or 500 g (1 lb) can **lychees**, drained and juice reserved

1¼ teaspoons **salt**

4 small round **aubergines**, quartered

50 g (2 oz) **green beans**, chopped into 2.5 cm (1 inch) lengths

6 **lime leaves**, torn

20 g (¾ oz) **krachai** or **galangal**, unpeeled

4 **baby sweetcorn**

15 g (½ oz) **green peppercorns**

2 large **green chillies**

2 teaspoons **sugar**

20 g (¾ oz) **cucumber**, diced

Forest curry with lychees

Although lychees are more likely to feature on a dessert menu, they work incredibly well in this fragrant vegetable curry. Try to find fresh lychees if possible.

1 Heat the water in a saucepan, add the curry paste and stir to blend thoroughly. If you are using canned lychees, add the reserved juice now, then add the salt and bring to the boil, stirring.

2 Lower the heat to a slow boil and add all the other ingredients except the lychees and cucumber. Stir for 30 seconds.

3 Add the lychees and cucumber and then cook the curry, stirring occasionally, for 3–4 minutes.

PREP **10**

COOK **8**

SERVES **4**

fruity

Dry banana curry

In Thailand there are 28 varieties of gluay, the generic term for banana or plantain. If you prefer to use plantain for this recipe, you will need the smallish, orangey-pink-skinned kind, not the large green-skinned ones.

1 Bring the coconut milk and curry paste to the boil in a saucepan or wok and simmer, stirring, for 3–4 minutes.

2 Add the banana and 3 of the lime leaves and cook for 4–5 minutes. Garnish with the remaining lime leaves, cut into thin strips.

300 ml (½ pint) **coconut milk**

1 heaped tablespoon **Panang curry paste** (see page 16)

4 unripe **bananas**, peeled and quartered

5 **lime leaves**

PREP
3

COOK
9

SERVES
4

simple

Thai yellow curry with carrot

150 ml (¼ pint) **vegetable stock**

8 **lime leaves**

25 g (1 oz) fresh **galangal** or fresh **root ginger**, peeled and sliced

175 g (6 oz) **carrots**, cut into chunks

2 large **red** and **green chillies**

4 **garlic cloves**, crushed

1 tablespoon **groundnut oil**

2 tablespoons crushed **roasted peanuts**

300 ml (½ pint) **coconut milk**

2 tablespoons **yellow curry paste** (see page 147)

8 canned **straw mushrooms**, drained

4 **shallots**

salt

This is a vegetarian version of the classic Thai yellow curry dish, with carrots adding a hint of sweetness.

1 Put the stock in a saucepan, add 5 of the lime leaves, the galangal or ginger, carrots, chillies and half the garlic. Simmer for 15 minutes. Strain the stock, reserving the liquid and both the carrots and chillies separately.

2 Heat the oil in a saucepan and fry the remaining garlic for 1 minute. Add the reserved carrot and the peanuts and cook, stirring, for 1 minute. Add the coconut milk and curry paste and stir until well blended. Add the reserved liquid, the mushrooms and shallots and simmer, stirring occasionally, for 15 minutes or until the shallots are cooked. Season with salt to taste.

3 Deseed and finely slice the reserved chillies. Use as a garnish for the curry, with the remaining lime leaves.

PREP **15** COOK **40** SERVES **2** hot

Minted green mung bean curry

A large proportion of India's Hindu population is vegetarian, so beans and lentils make up an important part of the diet. The addition of coconut milk gives this spicy, wholesome curry a delicious richness.

1 Place the mung beans, chilli powder and turmeric in a large saucepan with the measured water. Bring to the boil, cover, reduce the heat and cook gently for 20–25 minutes. Add the potatoes and continue to cook for 12–15 minutes or until tender.

2 Stir in the coconut milk, tomatoes and green chilli and cook gently for 4–5 minutes. Stir in the palm sugar and cook for 2–3 minutes until dissolved.

3 Remove from the heat, stir in the chopped herbs, season and serve immediately.

250 g (8 oz) **green mung beans**

1 teaspoon **chilli powder**

½ teaspoon **turmeric**

750 ml (1¼ pints) **water**

2 **potatoes**, diced

150 ml (¼ pint) half-fat **coconut milk**

2 **plum tomatoes**, roughly chopped

1 **green chilli**, deseeded and finely chopped

1–2 teaspoons grated **palm sugar** or **soft brown sugar**

small handful roughly chopped **mint leaves** and **coriander leaves**

salt

PREP
5

COOK
50

SERVES
4

spicy

1 tablespoon **tamarind paste**

4 tablespoons **water**

½ teaspoon **fenugreek seeds**

2 **dried red chillies**

100 g (3½ oz) freshly grated **coconut**

½ teaspoon **turmeric**

2 tablespoons **sunflower oil**

1 tablespoon **mustard seeds**

1 teaspoon **cumin seeds**

8–10 **curry leaves**

500 g (1 lb) **cucumber**, cut into 1 cm (½ inch) dice

salt

Cucumber and coconut curry

Mild-tasting cucumber is complemented perfectly by hot chillies, fragrant spices, tart tamarind and rich, sweet coconut in this utterly delectable stir-fry. Serve as a vegetable accompaniment with meat or fish dishes.

1 Mix the tamarind paste with the measured water and set aside.

2 In a frying pan, dry-fry the fenugreek seeds and red chillies for 1 minute over a low heat. Transfer them to a pestle and mortar with the tamarind mixture, half the coconut and the turmeric and pound to a coarse paste.

3 Heat the oil in a frying pan and when hot add the mustard seeds. As soon as they start to 'pop', stir in the cumin seeds, curry leaves and the coconut mixture. Stir and cook over a medium heat for 2–3 minutes, then add the cucumber. Continue to stir and cook for 5–6 minutes, then season well and sprinkle over the remaining coconut. Serve immediately.

PREP
10

COOK
10

SERVES
4

hot

Vegetable curry

All you need with this is some rice and warm nann bread, mango chutney and an ice-cold beer.

1 Heat the oil in a large saucepan, add the onion and fry until soft. Add the ground coriander, cumin, garlic and ginger and fry for 1 minute, stirring constantly. Add the tomatoes, measured water, chilli, potatoes, carrots, okra and cauliflower and a dash of salt and pepper.

2 Mix well, then cover and cook gently for 20 minutes, until tender. Stir in the coriander, then dish up on a mound of rice and with some warm nann bread.

2 tablespoons **vegetable oil**

1 **onion**, sliced

1 teaspoon **ground coriander**

2 teaspoons **ground cumin**

2 **garlic cloves**, crushed

5 cm (2 inch) piece of fresh **root ginger**, peeled and chopped

400 g (13 oz) can **chopped tomatoes**

150 ml (¼ pint) **water**

1 **green chilli**, deseeded and finely chopped

2 **potatoes**, cut into cubes

2 **carrots**, sliced

175 g (6 oz) **okra**, chopped

250 g (8 oz) **cauliflower florets**

2 tablespoons chopped **coriander leaves**

salt and **pepper**

PREP
30

COOK
30

SERVES
4

classic

125 ml (4 fl oz) **vegetable oil**

2 teaspoons **cumin seeds**

1 large **onion**, chopped

400 g (13 oz) can **chopped tomatoes**

1 tablespoon **ground coriander**

1 teaspoon **chilli powder**

1 teaspoon **sugar**

1 teaspoon **salt**

2 x 400 g (13 oz) cans **red kidney beans**, drained and rinsed

TO GARNISH:

coriander leaves

soured cream

Kidney bean curry

This is a nice, easy store-cupboard curry. Kidney beans add bulk and their robust nature means there is a lot of texture to this curry.

1 Heat the oil in a wok or frying pan, add the cumin seeds and chopped onion and fry until the onion is lightly browned. Stir in the tomatoes and fry for a few seconds, then add the ground coriander, chilli powder, sugar and salt and stir well. Lower the heat and cook gently for about 5–7 minutes.

2 Add the drained kidney beans, stir carefully but thoroughly and cook for 10–15 minutes. Garnish with coriander and serve with a dollop of soured cream.

PREP **15**

COOK **35**

SERVES **4–6**

hearty

Sayur kari

Sayur kari is an Indonesian vegetable curry, best served with rice. If yellow tofu is not available, use firm-textured tofu as found in many supermarkets and wholefood shops.

1 Heat the oil for deep-frying in a wok to 180–190°C (350–375°F), or until a cube of bread browns in 30 seconds. Deep-fry the tofu cubes, in batches, for about 1 minute, until they are crisp and golden. Remove with a slotted spoon, and set aside to drain on kitchen paper.

2 Drain off all but 2 tablespoons of oil from the wok and reheat. Add the shallots, chillies, garlic, ginger and lemon grass and fry over a gentle heat, stirring frequently, for 5 minutes, until softened.

3 Add the coriander, cumin, turmeric, chilli powder and shrimp paste. Fry the mixture for 1 minute. Stir in the stock and coconut milk. Bring to the boil and add the potato. Reduce the heat and cook the potato for 6 minutes. Add the beans and cook for a further 8 minutes.

4 Stir in the cabbage, bean sprouts and rice vermicelli, season with salt to taste and cook gently for a further 3 minutes. Stir in the fried tofu and serve.

PREP **15**

COOK **30**

SERVES **6**

healthy

2 tablespoons **vegetable oil**, plus extra for deep-frying

4 squares of **yellow tofu**, cut into 2.5 cm (1 inch) cubes

4 **shallots**, sliced

2 **green chillies**, deseeded and sliced

3 **garlic cloves**, chopped

1 tablespoon peeled and finely chopped fresh **root ginger**

1 **lemon grass stalk**, finely chopped

1 tablespoon **ground coriander**

1 teaspoon **ground cumin**

1 teaspoon **turmeric**

1 teaspoon **chilli powder**

1 teaspoon **shrimp paste**

600 ml (1 pint) **vegetable stock**

400 ml (14 fl oz) **coconut milk**

250 g (8 oz) **potato**, diced

125 g (4 oz) **green beans**, trimmed and cut into 1 cm (½ inch) lengths

125 g (4 oz) **white cabbage**, finely shredded

75 g (3 oz) **bean sprouts**

25 g (1 oz) **rice vermicelli**, soaked in boiling water for 5 minutes and drained

salt

2 large **onions**

125 g (4 oz) **ghee** or
2 tablespoons **vegetable oil**

4 **garlic cloves**

2 teaspoons **ground coriander**

½ teaspoon **turmeric**

500 g (1 lb) fresh **okra**, topped and tailed and cut into 1 cm (½ inch) slices

2 **tomatoes**, skinned and chopped

1 teaspoon chopped **mint**

½ teaspoon **garam masala**

salt and **pepper**

TO GARNISH:

sprigs of **mint**

Spicy okra

This mild curry, made with fresh okra, or ladies' fingers, and tomatoes, is both flavoured and garnished with mint.

1 Slice one of the onions very thinly. Heat the ghee or vegetable oil in a heavy-based saucepan and add the sliced onion. Fry gently until tender and golden brown.

2 Chop the remaining onion and place in a blender or food processor with the garlic, seasoning, coriander and turmeric. Process until the mixture is well blended.

3 Stir the blended onion and spice mixture into the fried onion in the saucepan and cook over a medium heat for 5 minutes, stirring occasionally.

4 Add the okra to the saucepan. Stir gently and then simmer, covered, for 20 minutes. Add the tomatoes, chopped mint and garam masala and simmer for 15 minutes. Serve garnished with mint.

PREP **10**　COOK **45**　SERVES **4**　mild

Cream cheese kofta curry

Paneer is the most widely used cheese in Indian cuisine. It has a soft consistency and many people make their own.

1 Boil the potatoes in some water with the green chilli, ginger and all but a pinch of the garam masala. When tender, drain the potatoes and mash with a little salt, the chickpea or gram flour, breadcrumbs and coriander seeds. Divide into 12 equal-sized portions.

2 Mix the paneer with the coconut and the remaining garam masala. Divide into 12 equal-sized portions. Flatten the potato portions and use to wrap around the paneer portions. Roll into balls, brush with beaten egg white and fry in the heated ghee or oil until golden brown. Drain and transfer to an ovenproof dish.

3 Add the bay leaves, chopped onions, garlic, cloves and peppercorns to the ghee or oil left in the pan and fry until golden. Stir in the yogurt, turmeric and chilli powder. Add the measured water and bring to the boil. Simmer for 10 minutes.

4 Pour this sauce over the koftas and cover with the tomatoes and coriander leaves. Cook in a preheated oven at 180°C (350°F), Gas Mark 4, for 10–15 minutes, or until heated through. Serve immediately.

PREP **30**

COOK **60**

SERVES **4–6**

creamy

1 kg (2 lb) **potatoes**, quartered

1 large **green chilli**, chopped

1 teaspoon peeled and grated fresh **root ginger**

½ teaspoon **garam masala**

2 tablespoons **chickpea** or **gram flour**

2 tablespoons fresh **breadcrumbs**

1 tablespoon roasted **coriander seeds**, ground

250 g (8 oz) **paneer**

1 tablespoon grated or desiccated **coconut**

1 **egg white**, beaten

175 g (6 oz) **ghee** or 3 tablespoons **vegetable oil**

2 **bay leaves**

2 **onions**, chopped

6 **garlic cloves**, crushed

4 **cloves**

6 **black peppercorns**

150 ml (¼ pint) **natural yogurt**

1 teaspoon **turmeric**

1 teaspoon **chilli powder**

300 ml (½ pint) **water**

500 g (1 lb) **tomatoes**, skinned and sliced

2 tablespoons chopped **coriander leaves**

salt

1 small **onion**, chopped

2 teaspoons peeled and grated fresh **root ginger**

5 **garlic cloves**, roughly chopped

2 **green chillies**, deseeded and chopped

100 ml (3½ fl oz) **water**

4 tablespoons **vegetable oil**

1 large **aubergine**, cut into 1 cm (½ inch) dice

500 g (1 lb) **potatoes**, cut into 1 cm (½ inch) cubes, boiled and drained

2 teaspoons **cumin seeds**

1 teaspoon **black onion seeds**

1 teaspoon **turmeric**

1 teaspoon **ground coriander**

1 teaspoon **ground cumin**

1 tablespoon **lemon juice**

salt and **pepper**

TO GARNISH:

chopped **coriander leaves**

Aubergine and potato curry

Aubergines cooked with potatoes and spices are wonderful stuffed into a sandwich or served with rice and tarka dhal.

1 Place the onion, ginger, garlic, chillies and measured water in a food processor or blender and process until smooth. Set aside.

2 Heat 2 tablespoons of the oil in a large frying pan and, when hot, stir-fry the aubergine until lightly browned. Remove with a slotted spoon and set aside.

3 Heat the remaining oil and, when hot, add the potatoes and cook until lightly browned. Remove with a slotted spoon and set aside.

4 Add the cumin and onion seeds to the pan, stir for 30 seconds, then add the turmeric, ground coriander, ground cumin and the onion paste. Fry for 2–3 minutes and then return the potatoes and aubergines to the pan. Season with salt and pepper and stir-fry for 3–4 minutes. Remove from the heat, stir in the lemon juice and serve hot, garnished with chopped coriander.

PREP **10**   COOK **12**   SERVES **4**   spicy

Egg and coconut curry

This is a quick and easy recipe that will liven up eggs for an interesting dinner dish.

1 Heat the oil in a saucepan, add the cinnamon, cardamom pods and cloves, and fry for a few seconds. As the spices change colour, add the onions, garlic, ginger and chopped chillies, and fry gently, stirring, until soft and golden.

2 Pour in the coconut milk and bring to the boil. Add the nutmeg, the slit chillies and salt, and simmer for 10 minutes or until the sauce is thick.

3 Add the eggs and simmer for a further 5 minutes. Transfer to a warmed serving dish and serve.

2–3 tablespoons **vegetable oil**

5 cm (2 inch) piece of **cinnamon stick**

6 **cardamom pods**

6 **cloves**

2 **onions**, finely chopped

2 **garlic cloves**, finely chopped

2.5 cm (1 inch) piece of fresh **root ginger**, peeled and grated

4 **green chillies**, 2 finely chopped and 2 slit

450 ml (¾ pint) **thick coconut milk** (see page 15)

¼ teaspoon freshly grated **nutmeg**

6 **eggs**, hard-boiled, peeled and halved

salt

PREP
10

COOK
25

SERVES
4

easy

1 tablespoon **sunflower oil**

2 **garlic cloves**, crushed

1 teaspoon peeled and finely grated fresh **root ginger**

2 tablespoons **medium** or **hot curry powder**

400 g (13 oz) can **chopped tomatoes**

1 teaspoon **palm sugar** or **soft brown sugar**

2 x 400 g (13 oz) cans **chickpeas**, rinsed and drained

salt

TO GARNISH:

natural yogurt, to drizzle

small handful of chopped **coriander leaves**

Chickpea curry

Chickpeas are an ancient food, eaten for millennia, and are a popular ingredient in Indian cooking. This classic curry uses canned chickpeas, so it takes virtually no time to cook and is perfect served as a vegetarian main dish.

1 Heat the oil in a large, nonstick wok or frying pan and add the garlic and ginger. Stir-fry for 30 seconds and add the curry powder. Stir and cook for 1 minute before adding the chopped tomatoes and palm sugar. Bring the mixture to the boil, cover, reduce the heat and cook on a medium heat for 10–12 minutes.

2 Stir in the chickpeas and mix well. Cook over a medium heat for 3–4 minutes. Season, then remove from the heat. Drizzle with the yogurt and sprinkle over the chopped coriander before serving.

PREP **5**

COOK **20**

SERVES **4**

hot

Coconut and potato curry

This fragrant, sweet, sour and spicy curry is flavoured with tamarind paste, palm sugar, asafoetida and curry leaves. If thinned down with some water, it also makes a great soup.

1 Heat the oil in a large frying pan and, when hot, add the mustard seeds, asafoetida, curry leaves, ginger and chilli. Stir-fry for 1 minute and add the potatoes. Sauté for 1 minute.

2 Sprinkle in the chilli powder and add the palm sugar, coconut milk and measured water. Bring to the boil and add the tamarind paste and cashews. Lower the heat and simmer for 10–12 minutes. Stir in the coriander leaves, season with salt and pepper and serve hot.

2 tablespoons **vegetable oil**

2 teaspoons **black mustard seeds**

¼ teaspoon **asafoetida powder** (see page 11)

8–10 **curry leaves**

1 teaspoon peeled and grated fresh **root ginger**

1 **green chilli**, chopped

500 g (1 lb) **potatoes**, cut into 2.5 cm (1 inch) cubes and boiled

1 teaspoon **hot chilli powder**

1 tablespoon **palm sugar** or **soft brown sugar**

200 ml (7 fl oz) **coconut milk**

250 ml (8 fl oz) **water**

1 tablespoon **tamarind paste**

2 tablespoons roasted **cashew nuts**, roughly chopped

3 tablespoons chopped **coriander leaves**

salt and **pepper**

PREP
10

COOK
15

SERVES
4

creamy

2 tablespoons **ghee** or **vegetable oil**

3 **garlic cloves**, crushed

1 teaspoon peeled and freshly grated **root ginger**

6 **spring onions**, sliced

1 tablespoon **medium curry powder**

½ teaspoon **black mustard seeds**

250 g (8 oz) **flat mushrooms**, thickly sliced

375 g (12 oz) peeled and cooked **potato**, cubed

1 teaspoon **salt**

1 teaspoon **garam masala**

150 ml (¼ pint) **thick coconut milk** (see page 15)

125 g (4 oz) **peas**

juice of ½ **lemon**

TO GARNISH:

1 tablespoon chopped **coriander leaves**

Mushroom, pea and potato curry

It is best to cook the potatoes whole and then cut them up, as this will stop them breaking up too much. You want a nice chunky consistency in the final dish.

1 Heat the ghee or oil in a heavy-based saucepan. Add the garlic, ginger and spring onions, and fry over a gentle heat, stirring occasionally, for 2 minutes or until softened.

2 Stir in the curry powder and black mustard seeds and cook for about 1 minute. Add the mushrooms, potato and salt, stir to combine, then cover and cook gently for a further 5 minutes, stirring occasionally.

3 Add the garam masala, coconut milk and peas and cook the curry uncovered for a further 4–5 minutes.

4 Stir in the lemon juice, taste and adjust the seasoning, if necessary, and serve at once garnished with coriander.

PREP **10**

COOK **15**

SERVES **4**

mellow

Shallot curry

The delicate, sweet flavour of shallots is complemented by the aromatic spices in this flavoursome curry.

1 Heat the oil in a large frying pan and, when hot, add the coriander and cumin seeds, tomatoes and shallots. Stir-fry for 2 minutes, then add the chilli powder, turmeric, ground coriander and cumin, sugar and lemon juice to taste. Stir to mix well.

2 Add the potatoes and water, cover and cook gently for 10–15 minutes, or until the potatoes are tender. Stir in the chopped coriander leaves, season with salt and pepper and serve hot.

2 tablespoons **vegetable oil**

1 teaspoon coarsely ground **coriander seeds**

1 teaspoon **cumin seeds**

3 **plum tomatoes**, roughly chopped

10 **shallots**, peeled

1 teaspoon **chilli powder**

½ teaspoon **turmeric**

2 teaspoons **ground roasted coriander**

1 teaspoon **ground roasted cumin**

1 teaspoon **sugar**

4–6 tablespoons **lemon juice**

3 large **potatoes**, cut into matchsticks

150 ml (¼ pint) **water**

2 tablespoons chopped **coriander leaves**

salt and **pepper**

PREP
10

COOK
20

SERVES
4

sweet

2 tablespoons **sunflower oil**

1 **onion**, chopped

2 **garlic cloves**, crushed

5 cm (2 inch) piece of fresh **root ginger**, peeled and grated

1½ tablespoons **red curry paste** (see page 16)

600 ml (1 pint) **vegetable stock**

3 **kaffir lime leaves**

250 g (8 oz) **sweet potatoes**, peeled and diced

250 g (8 oz) **pumpkin**, peeled, deseeded and cut into cubes

8 **baby sweetcorn cobs**

1 **aubergine**, roughly chopped

125 g (4 oz) **green beans**, chopped

125 g (4 oz) small **button mushrooms**

200 g (7 oz) can **bamboo shoots**, drained

salt and **pepper**

TO GARNISH:

1 tablespoon grated fresh **coconut**

handful of **Thai basil leaves**

Quick Thai vegetable curry

You can buy Thai basil leaves in Asian supermarkets. Kaffir lime leaves are available in most big supermarkets. Serve with jasmine or boiled rice.

1 Heat the oil in a large saucepan, add the onion, garlic and grated ginger and fry gently for 5 minutes, stirring occasionally. Stir in the Thai red curry paste and fry gently for 3 minutes, stirring constantly.

2 Add the stock and kaffir lime leaves and bring to the boil. Add salt and pepper to taste, then lower the heat and simmer for 2 minutes. Add the sweet potatoes and pumpkin, cover the pan and simmer for 10 minutes.

3 Next, stir in the sweetcorn, aubergine, green beans, mushrooms and bamboo shoots, replace the lid and simmer for a further 5–10 minutes, or until the beans are just tender but still crisp.

4 Taste and adjust the seasoning. Transfer the curry to a warmed serving dish and sprinkle with the coconut and basil leaves.

PREP **15** COOK **30** SERVES **4** quick

Mango curry

Use very ripe mangoes in this easy recipe to ensure a really fruity flavour.

1 Heat the oil in a large saucepan and, when hot, add the mustard seeds, sliced onion, curry leaves and dried chilli flakes. Fry, stirring, for 4–5 minutes, or until the onion is lightly browned.

2 Add the ginger and green chilli to the onion mixture, stir-fry for 1 minute and add the turmeric. Stir to mix well, then remove the saucepan from the heat.

3 Add the mangoes and yogurt, stirring constantly, until well mixed. Season with salt to taste. Return the saucepan to a low heat and cook for 1 minute, stirring constantly. Do not let it boil or the curry will curdle. Serve warm.

1 tablespoon **vegetable oil**

1 teaspoon **mustard seeds**

1 **onion**, halved and thinly sliced

15–20 **curry leaves**

½ teaspoon **dried red chilli flakes**

1 teaspoon peeled and grated fresh **root ginger**

1 **green chilli**, deseeded and sliced

1 teaspoon **turmeric**

3 ripe **mangoes**, peeled, stoned and thinly sliced

400 ml (14 fl oz) **natural yogurt**, lightly beaten

salt

PREP
10

COOK
10

SERVES
4

fruity

1 tablespoon **vegetable oil**

1 **onion**, halved and thinly sliced

4 **garlic cloves**, crushed

1 teaspoon **ground cumin**

2 teaspoons **ground coriander**

1 **green chilli**, finely chopped

6 **curry leaves**

400 ml (14 fl oz) can **coconut milk**

200 ml (7 fl oz) hot **water**

750 g (1½ lb) **pumpkin**, peeled, deseeded and cut into 5 cm (2 inch) cubes

2 tablespoons chopped **coriander leaves**

salt and **pepper**

Pumpkin curry

Coconut milk perfectly complements the spiced pumpkin in this creamy curry.

1 Heat the oil in a large saucepan and, when hot, add the onion and stir-fry until soft and lightly browned. Add the garlic, cumin, ground coriander, chilli and curry leaves and stir-fry for another minute.

2 Pour in the coconut milk, hot water and pumpkin, bring to the boil, cover and simmer gently for 10–15 minutes, or until the pumpkin is tender.

3 Season with salt and pepper and stir in the chopped coriander leaves. Serve hot.

PREP 10

COOK 20

SERVES 4

creamy

Aubergine pahi

This pickled aubergine dish is a favourite in many Sri Lankan households. It can be stored in the refrigerator for about a week, because the vinegar acts as a preservative.

1 Mix together the salt and turmeric and rub all over the sliced aubergines. Leave to drain for 2 hours.

2 Place the spice paste ingredients in a blender or food processor and blend to a thick paste. Set aside.

3 Place the ground coriander, cumin and fennel seeds in a pan and dry-fry, stirring, for 3 minutes. Leave to cool.

4 Pat the aubergine slices dry on kitchen paper. Heat about 1 cm (½ inch) oil in a heavy-based frying pan and cook the aubergine slices, in batches, in the hot oil for about 2 minutes on each side until crisp and golden. Remove with a slotted spoon and drain on kitchen paper.

5 Drain off all but 4 tablespoons of the oil and add the spice paste to the pan. Cook over a gentle heat for 5 minutes, stirring occasionally. Add the dry-fried spices, chillies, paprika and cinnamon. Cook, stirring, for a further 2 minutes.

6 Add the aubergine and the measured water. Cover and cook for 15–20 minutes, stirring. Stir in the sugar, serve.

2 teaspoons **salt**

2 teaspoons **turmeric**

500 g (1 lb) **aubergines**, very thinly sliced

1 tablespoon **ground coriander**

1 tablespoon **ground cumin**

½ teaspoon **fennel seeds**, crushed

vegetable oil, for frying

3 **red chillies**, deseeded and chopped

1 teaspoon **paprika**

½ teaspoon **ground cinnamon**

175 ml (6 fl oz) **water**

1 tablespoon **caster sugar**

SPICE PASTE:

1 **onion**, chopped

3 **garlic cloves**, chopped

2.5 cm (1 inch) piece of fresh **root ginger**, peeled and chopped

1 tablespoon **black mustard seeds**

150 ml (¼ pint) **malt vinegar**

PREP
20*

COOK
45

SERVES
4

spicy

* plus 2 hours draining

1 ripe **pineapple**

2 tablespoons **groundnut oil**

1 **red onion**, sliced

2 **garlic cloves**, crushed

2 **cloves**, bruised

5 cm (2 inch) piece of
cinnamon stick

¼ teaspoon **ground
cardamom**

½ teaspoon **turmeric**

2 teaspoons **ground cumin**

1 tablespoon **ground
coriander**

1 large **red chilli**, deseeded
and sliced

½ teaspoon **salt**

75 g (3 oz) **creamed coconut**
dissolved in 250 ml (8 fl oz)
boiling water

Pineapple and coconut curry

This fruity dish makes a good accompaniment to a beef or chicken curry.

1 Peel the pineapple, taking care to remove all the eyes. Cut the pineapple in half lengthways, cut away and discard the core and cut the flesh into 2.5 cm (1 inch) chunks.

2 Heat the oil in a flameproof casserole, add the sliced onion, garlic, cloves and cinnamon stick and fry over a gentle heat, stirring frequently, for about 5 minutes or until softened.

3 Add the ground cardamom, turmeric, cumin, coriander, chilli and salt to the pan, and fry for a further 2 minutes. Add the pineapple chunks and stir well to coat them evenly in the spice mixture.

4 Add the coconut milk, stir to mix and bring to the boil, then reduce the heat and cook the curry gently, stirring frequently, for 2–3 minutes or until the pineapple is tender but not mushy and the sauce is very thick. Taste and adjust the seasoning if necessary and serve immediately.

PREP
15

COOK
10

SERVES
6

fruity

Mild egg curry

The ginger and cinnamon add a lovely depth of flavour to this dish and the saffron complements this with its slightly bitter taste.

1 Heat the oil in a heavy-based saucepan, add the shallots, garlic, ginger, cinnamon stick and chilli, and fry over a gentle heat, stirring occasionally, for 3 minutes. Stir in the dhana jeera, curry leaves, saffron and its water and the salt, and fry for a further 2 minutes.

2 Add the coconut milk to the pan, stir to combine the ingredients, bring the curry sauce to the boil and boil for 4–5 minutes, until the sauce has thickened slightly. Reduce the heat, stir in the eggs and simmer the curry gently for 2 minutes. Taste and adjust the seasoning if necessary.

3 Transfer the curry to a warm serving dish. Scatter over the chopped coriander and serve immediately.

2 tablespoons **vegetable oil**

2 **shallots**, chopped

2 **garlic cloves**, crushed

2.5 cm (1 inch) piece of fresh **root ginger**, peeled and finely chopped

5 cm (2 inch) piece of **cinnamon stick**, broken in half

1 large **red chilli**, deseeded and chopped

2 teaspoons **dhana jeera powder** (see page 17)

5 **curry leaves**

½ teaspoon **saffron threads** soaked in 2 tablespoons boiling water for 10 minutes

½ teaspoon **salt**

450 ml (¾ pint) **coconut milk**

4 **eggs**, hard-boiled, peeled and halved lengthways

TO GARNISH:

2 tablespoons chopped **coriander leaves**

PREP
25

COOK
10

SERVES
4

mild

3 tablespoons **vegetable oil**

25 g (1 oz) **flaked almonds**

2 **onions**, sliced

2.5 cm (1 inch) piece of fresh **root ginger**, peeled and grated

2 **garlic cloves**, sliced

1 teaspoon **turmeric**

2 teaspoons **medium curry paste**

4 **carrots**, thinly sliced

1 **cauliflower**, cut into florets

450 ml (¾ pint) **vegetable stock**

2 **courgettes**, sliced

125 g (4 oz) frozen **peas**

200 ml (7 fl oz) **coconut milk**

50 g (2 oz) **ground almonds**

3 tablespoons **double cream**

salt and **pepper**

Quick vegetable korma

You can use other vegetables, such as beans, broccoli, mangetouts and aubergine in this simple curry, then dish up with poppadums, basmati rice, nann bread and mango chutney for an Indian banquet.

1 Heat the oil in a large saucepan. Toss in the flaked almonds and fry gently for 1–2 minutes until toasted, then put on a plate.

2 Add the onions, ginger, garlic, turmeric and curry paste to the pan. Fry for 5 minutes.

3 Add the carrots and cauliflower and fry for another 5 minutes. Pour in the stock and bring to the boil. Turn down the heat, cover the pan and simmer for 20–25 minutes until the vegetables are tender.

4 Add the courgettes, peas, coconut milk and ground almonds, then simmer, uncovered, for 3 minutes. Stir in the cream and a pinch of salt and pepper. Sprinkle with the toasted flaked almonds and serve.

PREP **15** COOK **35** SERVES **2** mild

Mussaman potato curry

This fragrant curry is gorgeous with nann bread or rice and a leafy salad. Any left-over curry paste can be kept in a screw-top jar in the fridge for up to 3 weeks.

1 First make the curry paste. Remove the seeds from the cardamom pods and dry-fry the seeds with the coriander and cumin seeds and the cloves in a frying pan for 2 minutes. Tip all of the fried spices into a blender or food processor and blend with the rest of the curry paste ingredients to make a thick paste.

2 Heat the coconut milk in a large saucepan and add 2 tablespoons of the curry paste. Mix well, then heat until simmering.

3 Turn down the heat, add the potatoes to the saucepan and cook for 6 minutes.

4 Add the peanuts, onion, water, sugar and salt. Stir well so the sugar dissolves and continue to simmer, stirring, for 5 minutes.

5 Turn up the heat and let the liquid bubble until the potato is tender, then serve.

750 ml (1¼ pints) **coconut milk**

400 g (13 oz) **potatoes**, peeled and cut into even-sized pieces

50 g (2 oz) **roasted peanuts**, crushed

1 large **onion**, chopped

5 tablespoons **water**

75 g (3 oz) **palm sugar** or **soft brown sugar**

2 teaspoons **salt**

MUSSAMAN CURRY PASTE:

3 **cardamom pods**

1 teaspoon **coriander seeds**

1 teaspoon **cumin seeds**

2 **cloves**

6 small **red chillies**

2 **garlic cloves**, halved

1 teaspoon **ground cinnamon**

1 cm (½ inch) piece of fresh **root ginger**, peeled and chopped

3 **shallots**, chopped

1 **lemon grass stalk**, chopped

juice of ½ **lime**

PREP
8

COOK
25

SERVES
4

hearty

accompaniments

Spiced lemon rice

200 g (7 oz) **basmati rice**

1 tablespoon **light olive oil**

12–14 **curry leaves**

1 **dried red chilli**

2.5 cm (1 inch) piece of **cassia bark** or **cinnamon stick**

2–3 **cloves**

4–6 **cardamom pods**

2 teaspoons **cumin seeds**

¼ teaspoon **turmeric**

juice of 1 large **lemon**

450 ml (¾ pint) boiling **water**

sea salt

TO GARNISH:

chopped **coriander leaves**

A typical southern Indian favourite, this citrus-flavoured rice dish makes the perfect accompaniment to plain grilled fish or chicken.

1 Wash the rice in several changes of cold water, drain well and set aside.

2 Heat the oil in a nonstick saucepan; when it is hot, add the curry leaves, chilli, cassia or cinnamon, cloves, cardamom, cumin seeds and turmeric. Stir-fry for 20–30 seconds and add the rice. Stir-fry for 2 minutes, then add the lemon juice and the measured water. Cover tightly, reduce the heat to low and simmer gently for 10 minutes.

3 Remove the pan from the heat and leave the rice to stand, covered and undisturbed, for 10 minutes. Fluff up the grains of rice with a fork, then season and garnish with the chopped coriander before serving.

PREP **5**

COOK **25**

SERVES **4**

spicy

Aubergine and cashew nut rice

Aubergine is enjoyed in a great many ways in Indian cooking. Here the chunks of moist, juicy aubergine are in perfect contrast with the fluffy rice and rich, tender cashew nuts.

1 Wash the rice in several changes of cold water, drain well and set aside.

2 Heat the oil in a large, nonstick wok or frying pan and when it is hot add the shallots, mustard seeds, dried red chillies, curry leaves, cassia or cinnamon, cardamom and bay leaf. Stir and fry for 1–2 minutes, then add the drained rice. Stir gently to coat the rice with the spice mixture.

3 Add the aubergine and turmeric. Stir to mix well and pour in the measured water. Season well and bring to the boil. Cover tightly, reduce the heat to low and simmer gently for 10 minutes.

4 Remove the pan from the heat and leave the rice to stand, covered and undisturbed, for 10 minutes. Squeeze over the lemon juice, add the pepper, fluff up the grains of rice with a fork and sprinkle over the cashew nuts and coriander. Serve immediately.

300 g (10 oz) **basmati rice**

2 tablespoons **sunflower oil**

4 **shallots**, thinly sliced

1 teaspoon **black mustard seeds**

2 **dried red chillies**

6–8 **curry leaves**

2.5 cm (1 inch) piece of **cassia bark** or **cinnamon stick**

2–3 **cardamom pods**

1 **bay leaf**

200 g (7 oz) **aubergine**, cut into bite-sized cubes

1 teaspoon **turmeric**

600 ml (1 pint) boiling **water**

salt

TO SERVE:

juice of ½ **lemon**

200 g (8 oz) roasted **red pepper**, diced

50 g (2 oz) roasted **cashew nuts**

chopped **coriander leaves**

PREP
5

COOK
30

SERVES
4

mellow

225 g (7½ oz) **basmati rice**

15 g (½ oz) **unsalted butter**

1 tablespoon **vegetable oil**

1 **onion**, finely chopped

2 **dried red chillies**

6 **cardamom pods**, lightly crushed

1 **cinnamon stick**

1 teaspoon **cumin seeds**

2 **bay leaves**

1 teaspoon **saffron threads**, soaked in 1 tablespoon hot milk

475 ml (16 fl oz) boiling **water**

salt and **pepper**

TO GARNISH:

crispy fried onions (see page 14)

Saffron and cardamom rice

Flavoured with the aromatic spices cardamom and saffron, this fragrant rice dish makes a delicious centrepiece for any Indian meal.

1 Wash the rice in several changes of cold water, drain well and set aside.

2 Heat the butter and oil in a large, heavy-based saucepan and add the onion. Stir and cook over a medium heat for 2–3 minutes. Add the chillies, cardamom, cinnamon, cumin and bay leaves.

3 Add the rice to the pan and stir-fry for 2–3 minutes. Add the saffron mixture and boiling water, season with salt and pepper and bring back to the boil. Cover tightly, reduce the heat to low and simmer gently for 10 minutes.

4 Remove the pan from the heat and leave the rice to stand, covered and undisturbed, for 10 minutes. Fluff up the grains of rice with a fork and serve garnished with crispy fried onions.

PREP
20

COOK
15

SERVES
4

tasty

Tomato rice

This aromatic, delicately flavoured and coloured rice would make a good dinner-party dish.

1 Wash the rice in several changes of cold water, drain well and set aside.

2 Heat the butter in a large, heavy-based saucepan and, when melted, add the onion, garlic, cumin, peppercorns, clove and cinnamon. Stir-fry for 2–3 minutes.

3 Add the peas, tomatoes, tomato purée and rice and stir-fry for another 2–3 minutes.

4 Add the boiling water and coriander, season with salt and pepper and bring back to the boil. Cover tightly, reduce the heat to low and simmer gently for 10 minutes.

5 Remove the pan from the heat and leave the rice to stand, covered and undisturbed, for 10 minutes. Fluff up the grains of rice with a fork and serve.

225 g (7¼ oz) **basmati rice**

25 g (1 oz) **butter**

1 small **onion**, halved and thinly sliced

1 **garlic clove**, crushed

1 teaspoon **cumin seeds**

4–6 **black peppercorns**

1 **clove**

1 **cinnamon stick**

50 g (2 oz) frozen **peas**

200 g (7 oz) can **chopped tomatoes**

2 tablespoons **tomato purée**

475 ml (16 fl oz) boiling **water**

2 tablespoons chopped **coriander leaves**

salt and **pepper**

PREP
15

COOK
15

SERVES
4

light

625 g (1¼ lb) **basmati rice**

1 tablespoon **sunflower oil**

1 teaspoon **cumin seeds**

½ teaspoon crushed **coriander seeds**

1 teaspoon **black mustard seeds**

1 **red chilli**

½ teaspoon grated fresh **root ginger**

750 ml (1¼ pints) **natural yogurt**

8 tablespoons chopped **dill**

salt

TO GARNISH:

chopped **red chillies**

Yogurt and herb rice

Lightly spiced rice, tossed with herbs and yogurt, makes a tasty alternative to plain boiled or steamed rice. Yogurt is naturally cooling, so this dish is the ideal accompaniment to really hot and spicy curries.

1 Cook the rice according to the packet instructions until just tender, drain and set aside.

2 Heat the oil in a large, nonstick frying pan and when it is hot add the cumin, coriander and mustard seeds. As the seeds begin to 'pop', add the chilli and ginger, stir-fry for a few seconds and then pour this mixture over the rice and stir to mix evenly.

3 Whisk the yogurt until smooth and stir it into the spiced rice with the chopped dill. Season and serve the rice immediately with chopped red chillies to garnish.

PREP
5

COOK
10

SERVES
4

mild

Jeera rice

This simple rice dish, flavoured with cumin, makes a great accompaniment to any Indian meal.

1 Wash the rice in several changes of cold water, drain well and set aside.

2 Melt the butter in a large, heavy-based saucepan over a medium heat. Add the cumin, clove and cardamom and stir-fry for 30 seconds.

3 Add the rice to the pan and stir to coat in the spiced butter for 2–3 minutes. Add the boiling water, season with salt and pepper and bring back to the boil. Cover tightly, reduce the heat to low and simmer gently for 10 minutes.

4 Remove the pan from the heat and leave the rice to stand, covered and undisturbed, for 10 minutes. Fluff up the grains of rice with a fork and serve.

225 g (7½ oz) **basmati rice**

25 g (1 oz) **unsalted butter**

2 teaspoons **cumin seeds**

1 **clove**

2 **cardamom pods**, lightly crushed

475 ml (16 fl oz) boiling **water**

salt and **pepper**

PREP
15

COOK
15

SERVES
4

simple

2 tablespoons **light olive oil**

6 **spring onions**, very finely sliced

2 **garlic cloves**, finely chopped

750 g (1½ lb) cooked, cooled **basmati rice**

2 ripe **plum tomatoes**, finely chopped

250 g (8 oz) **mixed sprouted beans** (a mixture of aduki, mung, lentil and chickpea sprouts)

small handful of chopped **mint leaves**

salt and **pepper**

Rice with tomato and sprouted beans

The bean sprouts in this light and fresh stir-fried rice dish give it a crunchy bite, while the generous addition of garlic gives a rich, aromatic flavour.

1 Heat the oil in a large, nonstick wok or frying pan. When it is hot, add the spring onions and garlic and stir-fry for 2–3 minutes.

2 Add the cooked rice and continue to stir-fry over a high heat for 3–4 minutes. Stir in the tomatoes and mixed sprouted beans and continue to cook over a high heat for 2–3 minutes or until warmed through.

3 Remove from the heat, season and stir in the chopped mint leaves. Serve immediately.

PREP
15

COOK
10

SERVES
4

subtle

Coconut rice

Lightly spiced and fragrant with coconut milk, this rice dish is the perfect partner for fish or seafood.

1 Wash the rice in several changes of cold water, drain well and set aside.

2 Heat the oil in a large, heavy-based saucepan and, when hot, add the mustard and cumin seeds, curry leaves and dried chilli.

3 Add the rice to the pan and stir-fry for 1–2 minutes. Add the coconut milk and boiling water, season with salt and pepper and bring back to the boil. Cover tightly, reduce the heat to low and simmer gently for 10 minutes.

4 Remove the pan from the heat and leave the rice to stand, covered and undisturbed, for 10 minutes. To serve, fluff up the grains of rice with a fork and garnish with roasted cashew nuts.

225 g (7½ oz) **basmati rice**

2 tablespoons **vegetable oil**

2 teaspoons **black mustard seeds**

1 teaspoon **cumin seeds**

10 **curry leaves**

1 **dried red chilli**, finely chopped

100 ml (3½ fl oz) **coconut milk**

375 ml (13 fl oz) boiling **water**

salt and **pepper**

TO GARNISH:

roasted **cashew nuts**

PREP
30

COOK
15

SERVES
4

light

375 g (12 oz) **basmati rice**

3 tablespoons **ghee** or **vegetable oil**

1 large **onion**, thinly sliced

2 **garlic cloves**, finely chopped

6 **cloves**

6 **cardamom pods**, bruised

7 cm (3 inch) piece of **cinnamon stick**, bruised

½ teaspoon **black peppercorns**

10 **curry leaves** (optional)

10 cm (4 inch) piece of **lemon grass stalk**, halved lengthways

1 teaspoon **turmeric**

1 teaspoon **salt**

600 ml (1 pint) **thin coconut milk** (see page 15)

300 ml (½ pint) **vegetable stock**

50 g (2 oz) **sultanas**

25 g (1 oz) toasted **flaked almonds**

Sri Lankan yellow rice

It is the turmeric that gives this dish its distinctive colour. However, it also adds a peppery flavour to dishes.

1   Wash the rice in several changes of cold water, drain well and set aside.

2   Heat the ghee or oil in a large heavy-based saucepan. Add the onion and garlic, and fry over a medium heat, stirring occasionally, for 5 minutes or until they are golden.

3   Add all the spices to the pan, stir to mix and cook for a further 1 minute. Stir in the rice and salt, and mix so the rice grains are coated in the spicy oil. Cook for 2 minutes.

4   Stir in the coconut milk and stock, bring to the boil, then cover the pan and simmer the rice very gently for 20–25 minutes. (Do not remove the lid during this time.)

5   Lift the lid of the pan and check the rice. It should be cooked and all the liquid should have been absorbed. The spices should have risen to the surface, so carefully remove and discard them. Fluff up the grains of rice with a fork and gently stir in the sultanas.

6   Transfer the rice to a warm serving dish and scatter over the flaked almonds. Serve immediately.

PREP **10**   COOK **35**   SERVES **6**   **sweet**

Nasi minyak

The English translation for this tasty and filling dish is 'Fragrant ghee rice'.

1 Wash the rice in several changes of cold water, drain well and set aside.

2 Heat the ghee or oil in a saucepan, add the onion, cinnamon, cloves and star anise, and fry over a gentle heat, stirring, for 10 minutes or until softened but not coloured.

3 Add the rice, turmeric and salt, and cook, stirring constantly, for about 2 minutes. Pour in the measured water and bring to the boil. Boil, uncovered, over a moderate heat for about 5–8 minutes, stirring frequently until almost all the water is absorbed.

4 Reduce the heat to low, cover the pan with a tightly fitting lid and cook the rice gently for a further 10 minutes. Remove the pan from the heat and, working quickly, loosen the rice grains with a fork. Cover the pan with a clean, dry tea towel and allow the rice to cook in its own heat for a further 10 minutes. Serve hot, garnished with the hard-boiled eggs and fried shallots.

375 g (12 oz) **basmati rice**

3 tablespoons **ghee** or **vegetable oil**

1 **onion**, finely chopped

10 cm (4 inch) piece of **cinnamon stick**, broken in half

6 **cloves**

1 **star anise**

¼ teaspoon **turmeric**

½ teaspoon **salt**

600 ml (1 pint) **water**

TO GARNISH:

2 **eggs**, hard-boiled, peeled and quartered

2 **shallots**, sliced and crisply fried

PREP **5**

COOK **40**

SERVES **4**

filling

Nasi guriah

375 g (12 oz) **basmati rice**

125 g (4 oz) **creamed coconut**, chopped

750 ml (1½ pints) **boiling water**

7 cm (3 inch) piece of **lemon grass stalk**, halved lengthways

5 cm (2 inch) piece of **cinnamon stick**, broken in half

4 **curry leaves**

½ teaspoon **ground nutmeg**

¼ teaspoon **ground cloves**

1 teaspoon **salt**

pinch of **pepper**

This dish of Indonesian spiced coconut rice is the perfect accompaniment to hot meat dishes.

1 Wash the rice in several changes of cold water, drain well and place it in a large heavy-based saucepan. Dissolve the creamed coconut in the boiling water. Add the coconut milk to the rice along with all the remaining ingredients.

2 Bring the rice to the boil and boil, uncovered, over a moderate heat for 8 minutes, stirring frequently, until almost all the liquid is absorbed.

3 Reduce the heat to low, cover the pan with a tightly fitting lid and cook the rice very gently for a further 10 minutes.

4 Remove the pan from the heat and, working quickly, loosen the rice grains with a fork. Cover the pan with a clean, dry tea towel and allow the rice to cook in its own heat for a further 15 minutes. Serve immediately.

PREP
5

COOK
35

SERVES
6

spicy

Parsee pilau rice

This rich rice dish goes particularly well with rich Indian curries such as Lamb Dhansak (page 40) or Chicken Bhuna (page 64).

1 Wash the rice in several changes of cold water, drain well and set aside.

2 Heat the ghee in a wide, heavy-based saucepan. Stir in the cardamom pods, cloves, cinnamon stick and peppercorns, and fry over a gentle heat, stirring constantly, for 2 minutes until fragrant. Add the saffron threads and rice to the pan and fry, stirring constantly, for a further minute.

3 Add the salt, orange-flower water, if using, and the measured water. Stir well to mix. Bring to the boil, then reduce the heat, cover the pan and cook the rice gently for 15 minutes without removing the lid.

4 Remove the pan from the heat and, working quickly, loosen the rice grains with a fork. Stir the sultanas into the rice, cover the pan with a clean, dry tea towel and allow the rice to cook in its own heat for a further 5 minutes.

5 Just before serving, stir both types of nuts into the rice, then serve hot.

375 g (12 oz) **basmati rice**

2 tablespoons **ghee**

6 **cardamom pods**, bruised

5 **cloves**

7 cm (3 inch) piece of **cinnamon stick**, broken in half

¼ teaspoon **black peppercorns**, lightly crushed

¼ teaspoon **saffron threads**

¾ teaspoon **salt**

½ teaspoon **orange-flower water** (optional)

600 ml (1 pint) **water**

25 g (1 oz) **sultanas**

25 g (1 oz) roasted **cashew nuts**

25 g (1 oz) **pistachio nuts**

PREP
5

COOK
25

SERVES
4–6

rich

Mushroom pulao

25 g (1 oz) **unsalted butter**

3–4 **garlic cloves**, thinly sliced

1 teaspoon peeled and grated fresh **root ginger**

3 **spring onions**, thinly sliced

½ teaspoon **turmeric**

250 g (8 oz) **chestnut mushrooms**, thinly sliced

225 g (7¼ oz) **basmati rice**, rinsed and drained

2 tablespoons chopped **coriander leaves**

600 ml (1 pint) boiling **vegetable stock** or **water**

salt and **pepper**

Chestnut mushrooms have a rich, meaty flavour and this rice dish would work well served as an accompaniment to a vegetable curry.

1 Heat the butter in a large, heavy-based saucepan and, when melted, add the garlic, ginger, spring onions, turmeric, mushrooms and rice. Stir-fry for 2–3 minutes, then add the coriander. Season with salt and pepper, pour in the boiling stock or water and bring back to the boil. Cover tightly, reduce the heat to low and simmer gently for 10 minutes.

2 Remove the pan from the heat and leave the rice to stand, covered and undisturbed, for 10 minutes. Fluff up the grains of rice with a fork and serve.

PREP
20

COOK
20

SERVES
4

fresh

Spinach and chickpea pulao

Basmati rice has a delicate texture and flavour and you need to keep a close eye on the timings as it is easy to over-cook. This method effectively steams the rice so try to avoid the temptation to remove the lid during cooking.

1 Heat the butter and oil in a large, heavy-based frying pan and, when hot, add the onion. Cook over a medium heat until lightly browned, then add the cumin, coriander, garlic, ginger, spinach, chickpeas, rice and dill. Stir and season with salt and pepper.

2 Pour over the boiling stock and bring back to the boil. Cover tightly, reduce the heat to low and simmer gently for 10 minutes.

3 Remove the pan from the heat and leave the rice to stand, covered and undisturbed, for 10 minutes. Fluff up the grains of rice with a fork and serve.

15 g (½ oz) **unsalted butter**

1 tablespoon **vegetable oil**

1 **onion**, finely chopped

1 teaspoon **cumin seeds**

2 teaspoons **ground coriander**

2 **garlic cloves**, crushed

1 teaspoon peeled and grated fresh **root ginger**

100 g (3½ oz) **spinach**, finely shredded

400 g (13 oz) can **chickpeas**, rinsed and drained

225 g (7½ oz) **basmati rice**, rinsed and drained

2 tablespoons chopped **dill**

600 ml (1 pint) boiling **vegetable stock**

salt and **pepper**

PREP **15**

COOK **20**

SERVES **4**

hearty

300 g (10 oz) **basmati rice**

1 tablespoon **sunflower oil**

1 **onion**, finely diced

1 teaspoon peeled and finely grated fresh **root ginger**

1 teaspoon finely grated **garlic clove**

2 teaspoons **ground cumin**

½ teaspoon crushed **cardamom seeds**

2.5 cm (1 inch) piece of **cassia bark** or **cinnamon stick**

4 **cloves**

250 g (8 oz) boneless, skinless **chicken thighs**, cut into bite-sized pieces

200 g (7 oz) **shiitake mushrooms**, thickly sliced

100 g (3¼ oz) **green beans**, cut into 2.5 cm (1 inch) lengths

600 ml (1 pint) **chicken stock**

salt and **pepper**

Chicken and mushroom pulao

Tasty and sustaining, this richly flavoured rice dish is great as an accompaniment to a light and crunchy salad and, perhaps, some Date, Apricot and Raisin Chutney (see page 234).

1 Wash the rice in several changes of cold water, drain well and set aside.

2 Heat the oil in a large, heavy-based frying pan and add the onion. Cook over a medium heat for 10–12 minutes or until it is softened and lightly browned. Add the ginger, garlic, cumin, cardamom, cassia bark or cinnamon stick and cloves. Stir-fry for 2–3 minutes, then add the chicken and cook over a high heat for 5–6 minutes.

3 Stir in the mushrooms, green beans, stock and rice, season and bring to the boil. Cover tightly, reduce the heat to low and simmer gently for 10 minutes.

4 Remove the pan from the heat and leave the rice to stand, covered and undisturbed, for 10 minutes. Fluff up the grains of rice with a fork and serve.

PREP
10

COOK
40

SERVES
4

rich

Nasi kunyit

Glutinous 'sticky' rice is available from oriental grocers. This dish, which translates as Malaysian glutinous rice, goes well with Nonya curries from Malaysia.

1 Place the rice in a sieve and wash it thoroughly under cold water. Drain it and place it in a wide saucepan with the measured water, salt, turmeric, peppercorns and pandanus leaves, if using. Bring to the boil, stirring constantly, then reduce the heat, cover the pan and cook over a low heat for 15 minutes.

2 Place the coconut milk in a saucepan and heat it to just below boiling point. Stir the hot coconut milk into the rice, cover the pan again and cook the rice over a very low heat for a further 10 minutes until all the liquid has been absorbed.

3 Remove the pan from the heat and, working quickly, loosen the rice grains with a fork. Cover the pan with a clean, dry tea towel and allow the rice to cook in its own heat for a further 10–15 minutes. Serve hot, garnished with crisply fried shallots.

500 g (1 lb) **glutinous rice**

475 ml (16 fl oz) **water**

1½ teaspoons **salt**

1½ teaspoons **turmeric**

½ teaspoon whole **white peppercorns**, crushed lightly

2 **pandanus leaves**, bruised (optional)

475 ml (16 fl oz) **coconut milk**

TO GARNISH:

2 **shallots**, thinly sliced and crisply fried

PREP
10

COOK
45

SERVES
6–8

creamy

Ingredients

175 g (6 oz) coarse **semolina**

1 tablespoon **sunflower oil**

1 teaspoon **black mustard seeds**

1 teaspoon **cumin seeds**

1 **dried red chilli**

10–12 **curry leaves**

1 **onion**, finely chopped

1 teaspoon **garam masala**

1 **carrot**, finely diced

100 g (3½ oz) **peas**

10–12 **cherry tomatoes**, halved

600 ml (1 pint) boiling **water**

salt

TO GARNISH:

chopped **coriander leaves**

TO SERVE:

lemon wedges

Spiced vegetable semolina

This hearty dish, known as Uppama, is rather like a pilaf. It comes from the south-western state of Kerala, where there are many variations using different combinations of spices and vegetables.

1 Place the semolina in a large, nonstick frying pan and dry-roast it over a medium heat for 8–10 minutes or until golden brown. Remove from the pan and set aside.

2 Return the pan to the heat and add the oil. When it is hot, add the mustard seeds, cumin seeds, chilli, curry leaves and onion. Stir-fry over a medium heat for 5–6 minutes or until the onion has softened, then add the garam masala, carrot, peas and cherry tomatoes. Stir-fry for 1–2 minutes, add the semolina and the measured water.

3 Stir and cook for 5–6 minutes over a low heat, until the semolina has absorbed all the water. Season, and garnish with chopped coriander before serving with wedges of lemon to squeeze over.

PREP **5**

COOK **25**

SERVES **4**

spicy

Spinach dhal

No Indian meal is complete without a bowl of spicy lentil dhal, which is one of the staple dishes eaten throughout the country. This version is flecked with fresh, tender baby spinach for extra flavour, colour and texture.

1   Place the lentils in a large saucepan with the water, turmeric and ginger. Bring to the boil. Skim off any scum that forms on the surface.

2   Lower the heat and cook gently for 20 minutes, stirring occasionally. Add the spinach and chopped coriander, stir and cook for 8–10 minutes.

3   Meanwhile, heat the oil in a small, nonstick frying pan and when it is hot add the garlic, cumin and mustard seeds, ground cumin, ground coriander and red chilli. Stir-fry over a high heat for 2–3 minutes, then tip this mixture into the lentils. Stir to mix well, season and serve the dhal immediately with rice or nann bread.

250 g (8 oz) **red lentils**, rinsed and drained

1.2 litres (2 pints) **water**

1 teaspoon **turmeric**

1 teaspoon peeled and finely grated fresh **root ginger**

100 g (3½ oz) **baby spinach leaves**, chopped

large handful of **coriander leaves**, chopped

2 teaspoons **light olive oil**

5 **garlic cloves**, finely sliced

2 teaspoons **cumin seeds**

2 teaspoons **mustard seeds**

1 tablespoon **ground cumin**

1 teaspoon **ground coriander**

1 **red chilli**, finely chopped

salt

TO SERVE:

boiled rice or **nann bread**

PREP
5

COOK
30

SERVES
4

spicy

Lentil biriyani

75 g (3 oz) **mung beans**, soaked in cold water overnight

75 g (3 oz) **red lentils**, washed thoroughly

175 g (6 oz) **basmati rice**

4 tablespoons **ghee**

2 **onions**, thinly sliced

4 **garlic cloves**, crushed

1 tablespoon peeled and grated fresh **root ginger**

1 **red chilli**, deseeded and finely chopped

1 **green chilli**, deseeded and finely chopped

2 teaspoons **ground coriander**

2 teaspoons **ground cumin**

1 teaspoon **garam masala**

1 teaspoon **salt**

½ teaspoon **saffron threads** soaked in 2 tablespoons boiling water for 10 minutes

TO GARNISH:

½ quantity **crispy fried onions** (see page 14)

A range of aromatic spices combine with lentils and beans to create a wonderful alternative to dhal as a healthy accompaniment to your meal.

1 Rinse the soaked mung beans thoroughly and place them in a pan of cold water. Bring to the boil, cover the pan and boil rapidly for 10 minutes. Reduce the heat and cook for a further 20–25 minutes until the beans are tender. Drain and set aside.

2 Cook the red lentils and basmati rice in separate pans of salted boiling water for 10 minutes or until cooked. Drain the cooked lentils and the rice and set aside.

3 Heat the ghee in a frying pan, add the onion, garlic, ginger and both chillies, and fry over a gentle heat for 5 minutes until softened. Add the coriander, cumin, garam masala and salt, and fry, stirring, for 5 minutes more. Stir in the saffron with its water and cook for 1 minute.

4 Place the mung beans, lentils and rice in a large mixing bowl. Add the cooked onion and spice mixture and stir.

5 Transfer the rice mixture to a lightly greased ovenproof dish, cover and cook in a preheated oven, 200°C (400°F), Gas Mark 6, for 15–20 minutes to heat it through. Serve the lentil biriyani garnished with the crispy fried onions.

PREP
20*

COOK
75

SERVES
6

healthy

* plus overnight soaking

Kitchere

Rice is combined with lentils and spices to create a fragrant dish that is substantial enough to be serve as a lunchtime meal, with some warmed nann bread or chapattis.

1 Wash the rice in several changes of cold water, drain well and set aside.

2 Heat the butter and oil in a large, heavy-based saucepan and add the onion. Cook until lightly browned. Add the cinnamon, cloves, peppercorns, ginger, chillies, cumin, coriander, lentils and rice. Season and stir-fry for 3–4 minutes.

3 Add the water and bring back to the boil. Cover tightly, reduce the heat to low and simmer gently for 10 minutes.

4 Remove the pan from the heat and leave the rice to stand, covered and undisturbed, for 10 minutes. Fluff up the grains of rice with a fork and serve garnished with crispy fried onions and hard-boiled eggs.

225 g (7½ oz) **basmati rice**

15 g (½ oz) **unsalted butter**

1 tablespoon **vegetable oil**

1 **onion**, halved and thinly sliced

1 **cinnamon stick**

4–5 **cloves**

6 **black peppercorns**

1 teaspoon peeled and grated fresh **root ginger**

2 **green chillies**, deseeded and finely chopped

1 teaspoon **cumin seeds**

2 teaspoons **ground coriander**

100 g (3¼ oz) dried **split yellow lentils** (moong dhal), rinsed and drained

600 ml (1 pint) boiling **water**

salt and **pepper**

TO GARNISH:

crispy fried onions (see page 14)

hard-boiled eggs, peeled and quartered

TO SERVE:

nann bread or **chapattis**

PREP
30

COOK
20

SERVES
4

filling

2 tablespoons **light olive oil**

1 teaspoon **black mustard seeds**

1 teaspoon **urad dhal**

8–10 **curry leaves**

250 g (8 oz) **shallots**, finely diced

1 **red chilli**, deseeded and finely diced

100 g (3½ oz) freshly grated **coconut**

salt

Shallot thoran

This wonderful, fresh shallot thoran is a lightly cooked 'salad', or relish, that accompanies nearly every southern Indian meal to provide a crunchy contrast to the saucy 'wet' dishes.

1 Heat the oil in a non-stick frying pan and, when hot, add the mustard seeds. As soon as they start to 'pop', add the urad dhal and stir-fry for 1–2 minutes, until the dhal turns a golden brown.

2 Add the curry leaves, shallots and green chilli and stir-fry over a medium heat for 5 minutes or until the shallots have softened slightly. Add the grated coconut, stir-fry for 1–2 minutes, then remove the pan from the heat. Season and serve.

PREP
5

COOK
10

SERVES
4

fresh

Cucumber and mint raita

Cool, fresh and extremely versatile, this raita can be served as an accompaniment to almost any dish, snack or meal. The cool cucumber and yogurt mixture acts as a perfect foil, especially for spicy food.

1 Place the cucumber in a bowl.

2 Whisk the yogurt and sugar until smooth and add the chilli, mint leaves and lime juice. Season, pour over the cucumber and toss to mix well. Chill until ready to serve.

3 Sprinkle with the cumin seeds and chilli powder just before serving.

1 large **cucumber**, peeled, halved lengthways and deseeded, then finely sliced

250 ml (8 fl oz) **natural yogurt**

1 teaspoon **caster sugar**

1 **red chilli**, deseeded and finely sliced

large handful of chopped **mint leaves**

juice of ½ **lime**

roasted **cumin seeds** and **chilli powder**, to sprinkle

PREP
10

COOK
0

SERVES
4

fresh

175 ml (6 fl oz) **natural yogurt**

2 small **bananas**, sliced thinly

2 tablespoons toasted **desiccated coconut**

pinch of **chilli powder**

lemon juice, to taste

salt

Banana and coconut raita

This is a more unusual combination of ingredients but it works surprisingly well and the sweetness of the banana is a great complement to more robust, spicy curries.

1 Place all the ingredients in a serving bowl and mix gently to combine.

2 Season lightly with salt to taste and serve immediately.

PREP **10**

COOK **0**

SERVES **4**

fruity

Papaya and coriander raita

This cooling accompaniment could be made with fresh mango instead of the papaya.

1 Place all the ingredients in a bowl; mix gently to combine. Taste and adjust the seasoning, adding lime juice to taste.

2 Cover the raita and leave in the refrigerator for 30 minutes before serving to allow all the flavours to develop.

175 ml (6 fl oz) **natural yogurt**

½ ripe **papaya**, peeled, deseeded and diced

2 tablespoons chopped **coriander leaves**

½ teaspoon finely grated **lime zest**

1–2 teaspoons **lime juice**

salt

PREP
10*

COOK
0

SERVES
4

cool

* plus 30 minutes chilling

200 g (7 oz) ready-to-eat **dried dates**, stoned

100 g (3¼ oz) ready-to-eat **dried apricots**

1 tablespoon **tamarind paste**

3 tablespoons **tomato ketchup**

1 teaspoon **ground coriander**

2 teaspoons **golden caster sugar**

1 teaspoon **hot chilli powder**

1 tablespoon chopped **mint leaves**

250 ml (8 fl oz) **water**

50 g (2 oz) **raisins**

salt

Date, apricot and raisin chutney

A no-cook, flavour-packed sweet and spicy chutney that will liven up any dish you care to serve it with. The chutney can be stored in the refrigerator for up to 1 week.

1 Finely chop the dates and apricots and place them in a food processor with the tamarind paste, ketchup, ground coriander, sugar, chilli powder and mint leaves.

2 Add the measured water and pulse the mixture in the processor until combined but still slightly chunky. Scrape the mixture down the sides of the processor and pulse again for 1–2 minutes.

3 Transfer the date mixture to a bowl and stir in the raisins. Season, cover and chill until ready to serve.

PREP
10
COOK
0

MAKES
400 g
(13 oz)

spicy

Mango chutney

The concentrated flavour of dried mangoes makes this a particularly fruity-tasting chutney.

1 Drain the dried mangoes, reserving 300 ml (½ pint) of the soaking liquid. Cut them into 1.5 cm (¾ inch) pieces.

2 Place the chilli powder, cardamom pods, cloves, mustard seeds, coriander seeds, peppercorns and cinnamon stick in a large, heavy-based saucepan. Dry-fry the spices over a gentle heat, stirring frequently, for 2–3 minutes until fragrant.

3 Add the reserved mango soaking liquid, the chopped dried and the fresh mango, the garlic, salt and vinegar to the spices. Bring to the boil, then reduce the heat and simmer gently for 10 minutes, stirring occasionally.

4 Add the sugar to the pan and stir over a gentle heat until it has dissolved. Raise the heat and boil the chutney, stirring frequently, until it is thick. This will take about 40 minutes.

5 Ladle the chutney into sterilized jars, seal, label and store for up to 2–3 months.

250 g (8 oz) **dried mangoes**, covered in cold water and soaked overnight

1 teaspoon **chilli powder**

6 **cardamom pods**, bruised

3 **cloves**

1 teaspoon **black mustard seeds**

1 teaspoon **coriander seeds**, lightly crushed

5 **black peppercorns**, lightly crushed

1 small **cinnamon stick**, broken in half

375 g (12 oz) peeled and pitted **mango flesh**, cut into 1 cm (½ inch) cubes

1 large **garlic clove**, thinly sliced

½ teaspoon **salt**

300 ml (½ pint) **white wine vinegar**

375 g (12 oz) **caster sugar**

PREP **20***

COOK **55**

MAKES 1 kg (2 lb)

fruity

* plus overnight soaking

1 large, ripe **pineapple**, peeled, cored and chopped into small pieces

3 **shallots**, chopped

1 **green chilli**, deseeded and finely chopped

1 tablespoon peeled and finely chopped fresh **root ginger**

25 g (1 oz) **raisins**

125 g (4 oz) **palm sugar** or **soft brown sugar**

125 ml (4 fl oz) **malt vinegar**

¼ teaspoon **salt**

Pineapple chutney

Try this tangy chutney as an unusual alternative to classic mango chutney. Serve either with poppadums or as an accompaniment to curries.

1 First, place the prepared pineapple with all the other ingredients in a heavy-based saucepan. Cook over a moderate heat, stirring constantly, until the sugar has dissolved. Bring the mixture to the boil, then reduce the heat and cook on a steady boil for 8–10 minutes, stirring occasionally, until most of the liquid has evaporated and the chutney is thick.

2 Pour the hot chutney into sterilized jars, seal, label and store. Once opened, the chutney will keep well for 3–4 weeks in the refrigerator.

PREP
10

COOK
15

MAKES
475 g
(15 oz)

tangy

Coriander and coconut chutney

This fresh, flavour-packed herb, coconut and spiced chutney can be served with snacks, as a dipping sauce or as a relish to spoon over grilled and barbecued fish and meat. It will keep in the refrigerator for up to 1 week.

1 Place all the ingredients in a food processor and blend for 3–4 minutes until smooth.

2 Season to taste and pour into a jar or bowl, cover and chill until ready to use.

200 g (7 oz) chopped **coriander leaves**

100 g (3½ oz) chopped **mint leaves**

50 g (2 oz) freshly grated **coconut**

1 teaspoon peeled and finely grated fresh **root ginger**

2 **garlic cloves**, crushed

4–6 **green chillies**, deseeded and chopped

2 tablespoons **ground cashew nuts**

1 teaspoon **dried mango powder** (amchoor)

juice of ½ **lemon**

1–2 teaspoons **golden caster sugar**

150 ml (¼ pint) **natural yogurt**

salt

PREP
10

COOK
0

MAKES
400 g
(13 oz)

fresh

100 g (3½ oz) block of **tamarind**

400 ml (14 fl oz) hot **water**

75 g (3 oz) **palm sugar** or **soft brown sugar**

50 g (2 oz) **soft brown sugar**

½ **red pepper**, finely diced

6–8 **black peppercorns**

1 teaspoon **red chilli powder**

1 teaspoon **sea salt**

2 teaspoons **cumin seeds**

1 teaspoon **ground cumin**

½ teaspoon **garam masala**

Tamarind and red pepper chutney

This delicious sweet, sour and spicy chutney can be used as an accompaniment to many starters and snacks.

1 Place the block of tamarind in a saucepan with the measured water and bring to the boil. Reduce the heat and cook gently for 20 minutes until the tamarind has broken down and become pulpy. Remove from the heat and strain into a saucepan through a fine metal sieve, pressing down to extract as much liquid as possible.

2 Add the palm sugar and soft brown sugar (or all soft brown if no palm sugar is available) to the tamarind liquid along with the remaining ingredients. Cook over a low heat for 15–20 minutes, stirring often. Remove from the heat and allow to cool before pouring it into a sterilized jar. This chutney will keep for up to 2 weeks if stored in the refrigerator.

PREP
5

COOK
40

MAKES
250 g
(8 oz)

sweet

Quick lemon pickle

This quick pickle is made on the day you intend to use it, but it can be stored in an airtight jar or container in the refridgerator for 3–4 days. It makes a perfect accompaniment to any rice, lentil or vegetable dish.

1 Heat the oil in a nonstick frying pan and when it is hot, add the mustard seeds. When they start to 'pop', add the curry leaves and dried red chillies. Remove from the heat and add the vinegar and the chopped lemon.

2 Return the pan to the heat and cook over a medium heat for 3–4 minutes. Add the asafoetida, season well and remove from the heat. Allow the pickle to cool completely before serving.

1 tablespoon **sunflower oil**

1 teaspoon **black mustard seeds**

6–8 **curry leaves**

2 **dried red chillies**, roughly crushed

2 tablespoons **white wine vinegar**

300 g (10 oz) **preserved** or **pickled lemons**, roughly chopped

pinch of **ground asafoetida** (see page 11)

sea salt

PREP
5

COOK
5

MAKES
350 ml
(12 fl oz)

quick

Aubergine pickle

375 g (12 oz) **aubergines**, cut into 1 cm (½ inch) cubes

1 tablespoon **salt**

75 ml (3 fl oz) **vegetable oil**

1 teaspoon **turmeric**

1 teaspoon **ground cumin**

1 teaspoon **ground coriander**

1 teaspoon **split mustard seeds**

1 tablespoon **chilli powder**

5 cm (2 inch) piece of fresh **root ginger**, peeled and grated

4 **garlic cloves**, crushed

4 **red chillies**, deseeded and thinly sliced

4 **green chillies**, deseeded and thinly sliced

250 ml (8 fl oz) **white wine vinegar**

90 g (3¼ oz) **palm sugar** or **soft brown sugar**

Some Indian grocers sell split mustard seeds, but if these are unavailable, use ordinary mustard seeds instead.

1 Place the cubed aubergine in a colander, sprinkle over the salt and set aside for 30 minutes, to allow the moisture to be drawn out of the aubergine.

2 Heat the oil in a large, heavy-based sauté pan, add the turmeric, cumin, coriander, split mustard seeds and chilli powder, and fry over a gentle heat, stirring constantly, for 3 minutes, until fragrant.

3 Add the ginger, garlic, chillies and vinegar, and stir well. Simmer gently for 10 minutes, stirring occasionally.

4 Add the drained aubergine cubes and the sugar to the pan. Mix well and cook over a moderate heat, stirring occasionally, for 35 minutes, or until the aubergine is very soft and all the flavours are well combined.

5 Ladle the aubergine pickle into sterilized jars, seal and label. This pickle will keep well for 2–3 months.

PREP **20***

COOK **50**

MAKES 875 g (1¾ lb)

tangy

* plus 30 minutes draining

Mango and onion seed pickle

This pickle is really quick to prepare and makes a great addition to any rice and curry dish. Green mangoes are widely available from any good Asian greengrocer.

1 Place all the ingredients in a small saucepan and cook over a medium heat for about 10 minutes. Remove from the heat, stir and allow to cool.

2 When cool, pour into a sterilized jar and cover. It will keep for up to a week in the refrigerator.

500 g (1 lb) **green mangoes**, washed, stoned and cut into 1 cm (½ inch) pieces

2 teaspoons coarse **red chilli powder**

2 **garlic cloves**, finely chopped

6 tablespoons **golden caster sugar**

4 tablespoons **white wine vinegar**

2 teaspoons **black onion seeds**

2 teaspoons **sea salt**

PREP
5

COOK
10

SERVES
4

fruity

450 g (14½ oz) ripe **plum tomatoes**, deseeded and finely chopped

½ small **red onion**, finely diced

2 **garlic cloves**, finely diced

1 **green chilli**, deseeded if desired, very thinly sliced

small handful of chopped **coriander leaves**

juice of 2 **limes**

salt

Fresh tomato relish

Quick to prepare, and packed with summer flavours, this zesty, fresh relish resembles a salsa in its consistency. Serve it with almost anything from meat or fish kebabs and rice dishes to breads.

1 Place the tomatoes, onion, garlic, chilli and coriander in a bowl.

2 Squeeze over the lime juice, season, cover and allow to stand at room temperature for 30 minutes before serving to allow the flavours to develop.

PREP
5*

COOK
0

SERVES
4

zesty

* plus 30 minutes standing

Coriander and cumin-flecked roti

These flatbreads make a great alternative to chapattis for scooping up moist curries and fragrant rice. The finely chopped coriander leaves and whole cumin seeds give the breads a lovely appearance and fabulous flavour.

1 Mix together the flour, salt, cumin and coriander in a large mixing bowl. Add the oil and work it into the mixture with your fingers. Gradually add the measured water and knead for 5–6 minutes until smooth, adding a little extra flour if necessary. Cover the dough with a damp cloth and allow it to rest for 30 minutes.

2 Divide the dough into 16 portions and form each into a round ball. Roll out each ball into a 12–15 cm (5–6 inch) disc, lightly dusting with flour if required.

3 Heat a large cast-iron griddle pan or a heavy-based frying pan over a high heat. Cook the rotis, one at a time, for 45 seconds on one side, then flip over and continue to cook for 1–2 minutes until lightly browned at the edges. Remove and keep warm in a foil package as you continue to cook the rest.

400 g (13 oz) **plain wholemeal flour**, plus extra for dusting

1 teaspoon **salt**

3–4 teaspoons **cumin seeds**

2 tablespoons very finely chopped **coriander leaves**

2–3 tablespoons **light olive oil**

250 ml (8 fl oz) lukewarm **water**

PREP
10*

COOK
45

MAKES
16

classic

* plus 30 minutes resting

Nann

225 g (7½ oz) **self-raising flour**, plus extra for dusting

5 g (¼ oz) sachet fast-action dried **yeast**

1 teaspoon **sea salt**

1 teaspoon roasted **cumin seeds**

2 tablespoons **natural yogurt**, lightly beaten

1 tablespoon melted **butter**, plus extra for brushing

4 tablespoons lukewarm **milk**

vegetable oil, for oiling

TO GARNISH:

coriander leaves

Though readily available in supermarkets and shops, there is nothing like freshly made nann bread. You can also vary the flavourings used when you make your own.

1 In a large, warmed mixing bowl, mix together the flour, yeast, salt, cumin, yogurt and butter. Add the milk and knead to make a soft dough. Cover with a lightly oiled sheet of polythene and leave to rise for 25 minutes in a warm (not hot) place.

2 Turn the dough out on to a large board or surface lightly dusted with flour and knead for 3–4 minutes or until smooth. Divide the dough into 8 portions and roll each one into a ball.

3 With a rolling pin, roll each ball out into an oval or triangular shape, the size of a pitta bread.

4 Bush with melted butter and cook in batches under a preheated hot grill for 2–3 minutes on each side. Serve hot, garnished with coriander leaves.

PREP
10*

COOK
20

SERVES
8

classic

* plus 25 minutes rising

Bhaturas

Quick and easy to prepare, these deep-fried puris (puffed-up bread) are excellent served with any moist curry.

1 In a large mixing bowl, combine the flour, oil, yogurt and salt. Mix well and add enough water to make a soft dough. Cover with a tea towel and leave to rest for 15 minutes.

2 Turn the dough out on to a lightly floured board and knead well for 3–4 minutes or until smooth. Divide the mixture into 10 portions and roll up each portion into a ball.

3 Using a rolling pin, roll each ball into an 8 cm (3½ inch) disc.

4 Heat the oil for deep-frying in a large wok or deep frying pan to 180–190°C (350–375°F) or until a cube of bread browns in 30 seconds. Carefully slide 2–3 bhaturas into the pan. When the bhaturas puff up, turn them over and fry for 1 minute or until lightly browned on both sides. Carefully remove with a slotted spoon and drain on kitchen paper. Repeat until all the bhaturas are fried and serve immediately.

175 g (6 oz) **self-raising flour**, plus extra for dusting

1 tablespoon **vegetable oil**

1 tablespoon **natural yogurt**

1 teaspoon **salt**

2–3 tablespoons **water**

vegetable oil, for deep-frying

PREP **25**

COOK **10**

SERVES **10**

light

225 g (7½ oz) **atta** or **chapatti flour**

1 teaspoon **hot chilli powder**

1 teaspoon **cumin seeds**

½ teaspoon **turmeric**

1 teaspoon **salt**

1–2 tablespoons **water**

oil, for deep-frying

Spiced puris

These puris make a quick and tasty snack. They are made with atta or chapatti flour, a medium-grade wheat flour that is sold in Indian and Asian shops.

1 Put the flour, chilli powder, cumin, turmeric and salt into a large mixing bowl and add enough water to make a soft but not sticky dough. Knead until the dough is smooth and elastic.

2 Divide the dough into 16 portions and roll each one out to an 8 cm (3½ inch) disc.

3 Heat the oil in a large wok or deep frying pan to 180–190°C (350–375°F) or until a cube of bread browns in 30 seconds. Fry the puris in batches of 2–3. When the puris puff up, turn them over and fry until browned and crisp. Remove with a slotted spoon and drain on kitchen paper. Serve hot or at room temperature. They will keep for up to a week, if stored in an airtight container.

PREP
10

COOK
20

MAKES
16

spicy

Kulcha

Kulcha, like nann, is a leavened bread, the difference being that kulcha is grilled and nann is baked.

1 Sift the flour and salt into a large mixing bowl. Sprinkle over the yeast and make a well in the centre. Pour in the measured water and mix well to produce a firm dough

2 Transfer the dough to a floured work surface and knead for 10 minutes or until it is smooth and elastic.

3 Place the ball of dough in a large greased bowl and cover with oiled clingfilm. Leave the bowl in a warm place for 45 minutes or until the dough has doubled in size.

4 Knock back the dough and add both types of sesame seeds. Work them into the dough, then divide it into 8 equal portions. Roll out each portion to produce a 15 cm (6 inch) circle. Make a small cross in the top of each dough circle and brush with the melted butter.

5 Cook the kulcha 2 at a time, under a preheated hot grill, for 3–4 minutes on each side, brushing them with more melted butter when you turn them over. Serve hot.

750 g (1½ lb) **strong white flour**

1 teaspoon **salt**

15 g (½ oz) fast-action dried **yeast**

450 ml (¾ pint) lukewarm **water**

2 teaspoons **black sesame seeds**

2 teaspoons **white sesame seeds**

50 g (2 oz) **unsalted butter**, melted

PREP
20*

COOK
30

MAKES
8

simple

* plus 45 minutes rising

50 g (2 oz) **wholemeal flour**

50 g (2 oz) **plain flour**, plus extra for dusting

¼ teaspoon **salt**

75 ml (3 fl oz) **water**

Chapattis

Chapattis are thinner and lighter than nann bread so are a good choice if you're serving rice as well. They are also easy to prepare with just a few basic ingredients.

1 Place the wholemeal flour in a bowl. Sift in the plain flour and salt and mix to combine the 2 types of flour.

2 Make a well in the centre of the flour and pour in the measured water. Using a wooden spoon, gradually draw the flour into the well and mix to produce a soft dough

3 Transfer the dough to a lightly floured surface and knead for about 5 minutes, or until it is smooth and elastic.

4 Divide the dough into 4 equal portions. On a lightly floured surface carefully roll out each portion to produce a thin 15 cm (6 inch) circle.

5 Heat a cast-iron frying pan until it is very hot, then turn the heat down to low. Cook the chapattis one at a time for 1 minute on each side until golden-brown spots appear on the surface of each chapatti. Serve the chapattis hot.

PREP
20

COOK
15

MAKES
4

simple

Courgette pancakes and raita

These spicy little pancakes can be made in advance and warmed through in a low oven just before serving – so they're perfect for entertaining. Fresh, tangy raita makes a lovely contrast to the rich, melting taste of the pancakes.

1 Squeeze out and discard all the liquid from the grated courgette. Put the courgette in a mixing bowl with the coconut, gram flour, cumin seeds, chilli and coriander.

2 Add a little water to blend until you have a batter of dropping consistency. Season with salt.

3 Lightly brush a nonstick frying pan with the oil and set it over a medium heat. Ladle a spoonful of the batter into the pan and flatten it with the back of a spoon into a 10 cm (4 in) disc. Cook for 2–3 minutes, then flip the pancake over and cook for 2–3 minutes until lightly browned. Remove from the pan, transfer to a plate and keep warm, covered, in a low oven while you use up the rest of the batter.

4 To make the raita, place the mint, yogurt and sugar in a food processor and blend until fairly smooth. Season with salt and pepper. Serve with the courgette pancakes.

150 g (5 oz) **courgette**, coarsely grated

150 g (5 oz) **desiccated coconut**

150 g (5 oz) **gram flour**

1 teaspoon **cumin seeds**

1 **red chilli**, finely chopped

2 tablespoons finely chopped **coriander leaves**

salt

sunflower oil, for brushing

FOR THE RAITA:

8 tablespoons finely chopped **mint leaves**

6 tablespoons **natural yogurt**

1 teaspoon **caster sugar**

salt and **pepper**

PREP
10

COOK
8*

MAKES
4

rich

* plus 2 minutes per pancake

400 g (13 oz) **rice flour**

¼ teaspoon **baking powder**

1 **egg**

2 tablespoons **sunflower oil**, plus extra for brushing

½ teaspoon finely crushed **fenugreek seeds**

1 teaspoon **cumin seeds**

1 **onion**, halved and thinly sliced

2 teaspoons peeled and finely grated fresh **root ginger**

2 teaspoons finely grated **garlic**

1 **red chilli**, finely sliced

400 g (13 oz) cooked peeled **prawns** and **crayfish tails**

3 tablespoons chopped **coriander** and **mint leaves**

salt

TO SERVE:

Coriander and Coconut Chutney (see page 237)

Dosas with prawns and crayfish

These crispy, light pancakes, rolled around a hearty spiced filling, are an essential part of southern Indian dining. When filled, they can be enjoyed as a meal in themselves, served simply with Coriander and Coconut Chutney.

1 Make the batter for the dosas by putting the rice flour, baking powder, egg, 1 tablespoon of the sunflower oil, fenugreek seeds and salt in a mixing bowl. Pour in cold water, slowly, whisking all the time to give you a batter that is the consistency of double cream. Season, cover and chill for 3–4 hours.

2 Meanwhile, make the filling. Heat the remaining tablespoon of oil in a large frying pan and when it is hot, add the cumin seeds and onion. Cook over a gentle heat for 10–12 minutes or until the onion has softened, then add the ginger, garlic and red chilli. Stir and fry for 1–2 minutes before adding the prawns and crayfish tails. Stir and cook for 2–3 minutes, stir in the coriander and mint, season and remove from the heat. Set aside and keep warm.

3 Brush a medium-sized nonstick frying pan with oil and set it over a medium-high heat. Add a ladleful of the batter and swirl to cover the base of the pan evenly. Cook for 1–2 minutes, then flip and cook on the other side for 30 seconds. Repeat until all the batter has been used, keeping the pancakes warm. Spoon over the prawn mixture and serve warm with Coriander and Coconut Chutney.

PREP
10*

COOK
17**

MAKES
4

spicy

* plus 3–4 hours chilling

** plus 2 minutes per pancake

Onion, chilli and gram flour bread

Gram flour, or besan, is made from ground chickpeas and can be found in large supermarkets and Asian stores. It gives these tasty, spiced flatbreads a lovely nutty flavour.

1 Sift both the flours into a large mixing bowl and add the onion, red chilli, chopped coriander and cumin and onion seeds. Season and mix together. Gradually pour in the measured water and knead for 2–3 minutes on a lightly floured surface, to make a soft dough. Allow to rest for 5 minutes, then divide the dough into 8 portions. Shape each one into a ball.

2 Roll the balls out on a lightly floured surface to a 12 cm (5 inch) diameter disc.

3 Heat a large, flat griddle pan or nonstick frying pan until it is hot. Cook the rolled-out discs of dough, one at a time, for 30 seconds on one side; brush with a little oil, flip over and cook for 1 minute, moving the bread around. Then flip the dough over again to cook on the first side for 1 minute or until the bread is lightly browned on both sides. Remove and keep warm, wrapped in foil, while you cook the remainder. Serve warm.

150 g (5 oz) **plain wholemeal flour**

150 g (5 oz) **gram flour**

1 **red onion**, finely diced

1 **red chilli**, deseeded and finely chopped

1 tablespoon chopped **coriander leaves**

1 teaspoon **cumin seeds**

1 teaspoon **black onion seeds**

100–150 ml (3¼–5 fl oz) lukewarm **water**

salt

sunflower or **light olive oil**, for brushing

PREP **20**

COOK **20**

MAKES **8**

hearty

index

acknowledgements

Executive editor: Nicola Hill
Editor: Kerenza Swift
Executive art editor: Darren Southern
Designer: Ginny Zeal
Production manager: Ian Paton
Illustrator: Peter Liddiard, Sudden
Impact Media